k.d. lang

k.d. lang

PAULA MARTINAC

MARTIN DUBERMAN, General Editor

CHELSEA HOUSE PUBLISHERS ▨ Philadelphia

CHELSEA HOUSE PUBLISHERS

EDITORIAL DIRECTOR   Richard Rennert
EXECUTIVE MANAGING EDITOR   Karyn Gullen Browne
COPY CHIEF   Robin James
PICTURE EDITOR   Adrian G. Allen
CREATIVE DIRECTOR   Robert Mitchell
ART DIRECTOR   Joan Ferrigno
PRODUCTION MANAGER   Sallye Scott

LIVES OF NOTABLE GAY MEN AND LESBIANS
SENIOR EDITOR   Sean Dolan
SERIES DESIGN   Basia Niemczyc

Staff for **k.d. lang**
ASSISTANT EDITOR   Annie McDonnell
PICTURE RESEARCHER   Matthew Dudley
COVER ILLUSTRATION   Bonnie Gardner

Introduction © 1995 by Martin B. Duberman

Library of Congress Cataloging-in-Publication Data

Martinac, Paula, 1954–
k.d. lang/Paula Martinac.
p. cm.—(Lives of notable gay men and lesbians)
Includes bibliographical references (p.) and index.
ISBN 0-7910-2872-0
        0-7910-2899-2 (pbk.)
1. Lang, K. D. (Kathy Dawn), 1961– —Juvenile literature. 2. Singers—
Canada—Biography—Juvenile literature. 3. Gay musicians—Canada—
Biography—Juvenile literature. [1. Lang, K. D. (Kathy Dawn), 1961–
2. Musicians. 3. Lesbians—Biography. 4. Women—Biography.] I.
Title. II. Series.
ML3930.L175M37 1995   95-14170
782.42164'092—dc20   CIP
[B]   AC MN

FRONTISPIECE
Charismatic singer k.d. lang has become the first openly gay
musical superstar.

CONTENTS

Titles in
◧ LIVES OF NOTABLE GAY MEN AND LESBIANS ◨

ON BEING DIFFERENT

Martin Duberman

Being different is never easy. Especially in a culture like ours, which puts a premium on conformity and equates difference with deficiency. And especially during the teenage years when one feels desperate for acceptance and vulnerable to judgment. If you are taller or shorter than average, or fatter or thinner, or physically challenged, or of the "wrong" color, gender, religion, nationality, or sexual orientation, you are likely to be treated as "less than," as inferior to what the majority has decreed is the optimal, standard model.

Theoretically, those of us who are different should be delighted that we are *not* ordinary, not just another cookie-cutter product of mainstream culture. We should glory in the knowledge that many remarkably creative figures, past and present, lived outside accepted norms and pressed hard against accepted boundaries.

But in reality many of us have internalized the majority's standards of worth, and we do not feel very good about ourselves. How could we? When we look around us, we see that most people in high places of visibility, privilege, and power are white, heterosexual males of a very traditional kind. That remains true even though intolerance may have ebbed *somewhat* in recent decades and people of diverse backgrounds may have *begun* to attain more of a foothold in our culture.

Many gay men and lesbians through time have looked and acted like "ordinary" people and could therefore choose to "stay in the closet" and avoid social condemnation—though the effort at concealment produced its own turmoil and usually came at the price of self-acceptance. On the other hand, "sissy" gay men or "butch" lesbians have been quickly categorized and scorned by the mainstream culture as "sexual deviants"—even though no necessary link exists between gender nonconformity and sexual orientation. In the last 15 years or so, however, more and more people who previously would have passed as straight *have* been choosing to "come out." They sense that social consequences are no longer as severe as they once were—and that the psychic costs of concealment are taking too great a toll.

Yet even today, there are comparatively few role models available for gays and lesbians to emulate. And unlike other oppressed minorities, homosexuals don't often find confirmation within their own families. Even when a homosexual child is not rejected outright, acceptance comes within a family unit that is structurally heterosexual and in which homosexuality is generally mocked and decried. With his or her different desire and experience, the gay son or lesbian daughter remains an exotic. Moreover, such children are unable to find in family lore and traditions—as other minority people can—a compensatory source of validation to counterbalance the ridicule of mainstream culture.

Things are rarely any better at school, where textbooks and lessons are usually devoid of relevant information about homosexuality. Nor does the mainstream culture—movies or television, for example—often provide gays or lesbians with positive images of themselves, let alone any sense of historical antecedents. These silences are in large measure a reflection of the culture's homophobia. But to a lesser degree they reflect two other matters as well: the fact that many accomplished gay men and lesbians in the past refused to publicly acknowledge their sexuality (sometimes even to themselves); and secondly, the problem of assigning "gay" or "lesbian" identities to past figures who lived at a time when those conceptual categories did not exist.

For the surprising finding of recent scholarship is that categorizing human beings on the basis of sexual desire alone is a relatively recent phenomenon of the last several hundred years. It is a development, many historians believe, tied to the increasing urbanization of Europe and the Americas, and to the new opportunities city life presented for anonymity—for freedom from the relentless scrutiny of family and neighbors that had characterized farming communities and small towns. Only with the new freedom afforded by city life, historians are telling us, could people who felt they were different give free rein to their natures, lay claim to a distinctive identity, and begin to elaborate a subculture that would reflect it.

Prior to, say, 1700 (the precise date is under debate), the descriptive categories of "straight" or "gay" were not widely employed in dividing up human nature. Even today, in many non-Western parts of the world, it is unusual to categorize people on the basis of sexual orientation alone. Through time and across cultures it has often been assumed that *both* same- and opposite-gender erotic feelings (what we now call "bisexuality") could coexist in an individual—even if *acting* on same-gender impulses was usually taboo.

In the West, where we *do* currently divide humanity into oppositional categories of "gay" and "straight," most people grow up accepting that division as "natural" and dutifully assign themselves to one category or the other. Those who adopt the definition "gay" or "lesbian," however, soon discover that mainstream culture offers homosexuals (unlike heterosexuals) no history or sense of forebears. This is a terrible burden, especially during the teenage years, when one is actively searching for a usable identity, for a continuum in which to place oneself and lay claim to a contented and productive life.

This series is designed, above all, to fill that huge, painful cultural gap. It is designed to instill not only pride in antecedents but encouragement, the kind of encouragement that literature and biography have always provided: proof that someone else out there has felt what we have felt, experienced what we have experienced, been where we have been—and has endured, achieved, and flourished.

But *who* to include in this series has been problematic. Even today, many people refuse to define themselves as gay or lesbian. In some cases, they do not wish to confine what they view as their fluid sexuality into narrow, either/or categories. In other cases, they may acknowledge to themselves that their sexuality does fit squarely within the "gay" category, yet refuse to say so publicly, unwilling to take on the onus of a lesbian or gay identity. In still other cases, an individual's sense of sexual identity can change during his or her lifetime, as can his or her sense of its importance, when compared with many other strands, in defining their overall temperament.

Complicating matters still further is the fact that even today—when multitudes openly call themselves gay or lesbian, and when society as a whole argues about gay marriage and parenting or the place of gay people in the military—there is still no agreed-upon definition of what centrally constitutes a gay or lesbian identity. Should we call someone gay if his or her sexual desire is *predominantly* directed toward people of their own gender? But then how do we establish predominance? And by "desire" do we mean actual behavior—or fantasies that are never acted out? (Thus Father John McNeill, the writer and Jesuit, has insisted—though he has never actually had sex with another man—that on the basis of his erotic fantasies, he *is* a gay man.)

Some scholars and theorists even argue that genital sexuality need not be present in a relationship before we can legitimately call it gay or lesbian, stressing instead the central importance of same-gender *emotional* commitment. The problem of definition is then further complicated when we include the element of *self*-definition. If we come across someone in the past who does not explicitly self-identify as gay, by what right, and according to what evidence, can we claim them anyway?

Should we eliminate all historical figures who lived before "gay" or "lesbian" were available categories for understanding and ordering their experience? Are we entitled, for the purposes of this series, to include at least some of those from the past whose sexuality seems not to have been confined to one gender or the other, or who—as a cover, to protect a public image or a career—may have married, and thus have been commonly taken to be heterosexual? And if we do not include some of those whose sexuality cannot be clearly categorized as "gay," then how can we speak of a gay and lesbian continuum, a *history*?

In deciding which individuals to include in *Notable Gay Men and Lesbians,* I have gone back and forth between these competing definitions, juggling, combining, and, occasionally, finessing them. For the most part, I have tried to confine my choices to those figures who *by any definition* (same-gender emotional commitment, erotic fantasy, sexual behavior, *and* self-definition) do clearly qualify for inclusion.

But alas, we often lack the needed intimate evidence for such clear-cut judgments. I have regretfully omitted from the series many bisexual figures, and especially the many well-known women—Tallulah Bankhead, Judy Garland, Greta Garbo, or Josephine Baker, for example—whose erotic and emotional preference seem indeterminable (usually for lack of documentation). But I will probably also include a few—Margaret Mead, say, or Marlene Dietrich—as witnesses to the difficult ambiguities of sexual definition, and to allow for a discussion of those ambiguities.

In any case, I suspect much of the likely criticism over this or that choice will come from those eager to conceal their distaste for a series devoted to "Notable (no less!) Gay Men and Lesbians" under the guise of protesting a single inclusion or omission within it. That kind of criticism can be easily borne, and is more than compensated for, by the satisfaction of acquainting today's young gays and lesbians—and indeed all who feel "different"—with knowledge of some of those distinguished forebears whose existence can inform and comfort them.

⬧   ⬧   ⬧

When the musician k.d. lang publicly came out as a lesbian in 1992, the gesture seemed epochal. Many so-called "ordinary" gay men and lesbians had been out and politically active for decades, but in the entertainment industry, no one is supposed to be ordinary—except in regard to his or her sexual preference.

k.d. lang was in fact the very first major female recording artist publicly to acknowledge her sexual preference. She would claim never to have been *in* the closet. And indeed, she had never denied her lesbianism, had included hints of it in her lyrics, and had presented an androgynous appearance—though these are not the equivalents, of course, of an overt declaration.

It is far from clear that lang's burgeoning career could earlier have survived an explicit avowal of lesbianism. A poll in *Rolling Stone* magazine as late as 1988 revealed that a full 75 percent of its readership regarded homosexuality as unacceptable in friends and co-workers. lang's decision to come out was thus audacious, its potential consequences on her career unpredictable—even if by 1992 she had four successful albums and two Grammy awards behind her.

But though she could not have known it in advance, her coming out had no significant negative consequences and her career has since soared. This, in turn, has given courage to a number of other prominent performers—of whom Melissa Etheridge and Elton John are the best known—to be equally forthright.

And as Paula Martinac points out in this colorful, empathic biography of lang, honesty has proven emancipatory for lang herself: It was, lang has said, "like an emotional veil had been taken away." lang has no wish, however, to become a public spokesperson for the gay movement nor to subsume the many facets of her personality and interests under the label "Lesbian."

Her historic coming-out has provided millions of young women with a much-needed role model. That alone, Martinac compellingly argues, has been an "extremely political" act. But lang is above all a musician and a performer, and she wants to continue to center her energies on her music.

As a singer and songwriter, lang's recent break with country music and her experimentations with jazz and pop suggest a career with many creative turns ahead. And it is of course possible, too, that an analogous evolution will take place in her politics. As Martinac points out, the "'I'm an artist, not an activist' line has grated on a lot of nerves." And it has already become clear that lang has moved beyond that position. In the interviews she has given since coming out in 1992, she has been markedly more open in discussing her personal life, and in a parallel shift, has accelerated her involvement in the struggle against AIDS.

Martinac quotes lang as saying, "One of my goals is to keep dissatisfied." The rebelliousness that has marked her temperament from the beginning—and which is traced so vividly in this biography—promises to produce many more turns and surprises in the years ahead.

CHAPTER ONE

THE "L WORD"

There's something I've been wanting to tell you for a while. I'm a L-L-L-Lawrence Welk fan.

At Radio City Music Hall, the audience roared as a shower of champagne bubbles began to drift across the stage. "Women were howling," a fan later commented, describing the tone of the August 1992 concert. Only two months earlier, in an exclusive interview with the national gay magazine, the *Advocate,* country and pop singer k.d. lang had put to rest the speculations and conjectures about her sexual orientation that had dogged her for years. "I want to be out!" she announced to *Advocate* interviewer Brendan Lemon. And then on the New York City stage, before thousands of her fans, she teased and toyed with her very public coming out as a lesbian. "I try to deal with my sexuality in a humorous way," she had told Lemon, "because that's how I feel comfortable."

k.d. lang—performer, personality, often heralded as the best voice of her generation—was out of the closet, the first major female recording artist to acknowledge

When she came out in 1992, k.d. lang was prepared for a negative reaction, but the androgynous performer has become more popular than ever. "k.d. lang," wrote *New York Times* reporter Michael Specter, "is the type of politically radical vegetarian lesbian defender of wildlife you'd want to bring home to mother."

her sexual orientation in public, thus paving the way for others. Yet she would later maintain that she had never really been in the closet. Almost a decade earlier, she had made her first appearances in small Canadian music venues, sporting a spiky haircut and a butch demeanor and singing songs with "I-you" lyrics instead of gender-specific ones. Lesbians spotted her as one of their own from the very beginning, but she chose not to make a public declaration about her sexuality. In lang's view, as long as she did not deny anything, she was not closeted. When curious interviewers quizzed her about marriage and lovers, she asked them to move on to the next question, stating that what she really wanted to discuss was her art, not her private life.

Over the years, she had been approached several times by the *Advocate* for an interview but always said no. Later, she acknowledged that it had taken her "a long time to say yes to the gay press" because of the implications of doing so and the fear of facing the inevitable question—"Are you or have you ever been . . . ?"

But by 1992, with four albums and two Grammy awards behind her, and a devoted following that cut across the lines of gender and age, lang could afford to risk addressing the question head-on. "k.d. lang and myself, we came out after a certain amount of success," notes rock singer Melissa Etheridge, "after we'd broken through a lot of the barriers and climbed a lot of the difficult parts of building a career." No openly lesbian vocalist had ever managed to achieve superstar status, and had lang come out before she achieved celebrity, "She would have just been Phranc [the lesbian folk singer]," one fan hypothesizes.

lang knew that if she didn't make the statement about her orientation herself, someone else would soon make it for her. "Outing," the practice of disclosing a public figure's homosexuality without their consent, had begun in 1989 as a tactic used by gay activists in the United States who were fed up with closeted public officials who were actively harming the lesbian and gay civil rights movement and the fight against AIDS by their collaboration with the Republican administration. But outing had quickly broadened to target all celebrity lesbians and gay men who did not publicly acknowledge their sexual orientation. A controversial issue in the gay community, outing was upheld by those

Pop star Elton John (left) is one of the well-known entertainers to have come out of the closet in the wake of lang's pioneering disclosure. Even some less-established performers, such as RuPaul, now feel comfortable being up front about their sexuality.

who considered it a journalist's right and duty to explore all aspects of a celebrity's life. "'Outing' is a primarily journalistic movement to treat homosexuality as equal to heterosexuality in the media," wrote gay publisher Gabriel Rotello in his magazine *Outweek*. Gay activists were clear about what they wanted from celebrities: nothing short of saying the "L word" or the "G word" would suffice. After being supported financially and emotionally by their lesbian and gay fans for years, famous "closet cases" could either come out or be dragged out.

A significant number in the lesbian and gay community decried outing as a hostile and unnecessary invasion of privacy. Gretchen Phillips, an openly lesbian musician from the group Two Nice Girls, found the gay press's anger misplaced and thought it should "trash the homophobes because that's where the problem is. Gay performers aren't doing anything wrong."

The mainstream tabloid press was also rife with rumors of the gay love lives of the stars, and celebrities like Whitney Houston and Richard Gere had not stilled the gossip with heterosexual marriages. The media frenzy that accompanied Martina Navratilova's messy breakup with lover Judy Nelson forced the tennis champion formally out of the closet.

Ultimately, lang realized that she would have to own her sexual orientation, not just remain silent about it. She did not want "to have to act defensively because of some tabloid atrocity." lang came out

Like lang, flamboyant singer Boy George had playfully cross-dressed and toyed with gender roles for years before publicly acknowledging his homosexuality.

publicly "to alleviate a lot of personal pressure," to help the gay community by "broadening the acceptability walls," and to be responsible to herself by being completely honest.

lang had no way of knowing at the time of the *Advocate* interview that her coming out would be easy and painless, that she would be as popular as an openly lesbian performer as she was as an androgynous one. She had already met with a lot of implicit homophobia in the country music arena, where radio stations refused to give her much airplay even after her hit country album had won a Grammy. Successful gay musicians such as Elton John, Boy George, and Melissa Etheridge had not made any moves to come out—why should she risk everything to be a path-breaker? "My career could have been over. In the industry, they thought that would happen to me," she recalls. It was not an unreasonable fear. A disturbing poll in *Rolling Stone* magazine as late as 1988 indicated that 75 percent of its readers did not consider homosexuality "acceptable" in friends and co-workers. What would the record-buying public think of a lesbian k.d. lang?

And what would her record company think? "This is a very conservative country," mused Howie Klein, vice president of Sire Records, lang's label, "and record companies like to steer away from potential controversy."

But lang's biggest fear in coming out concerned her mother, who still lives in the small Canadian town where lang grew up and who had repeatedly requested that her daughter remain silent on the issue of sexual orientation. "When I did it," lang recalls, "I called her and we had a cry. . . . I think she thought people would be more negative than they were."

Ultimately, lang's fears were unfounded. Her record company waited for negative fallout that did not occur. Public reaction to her coming-out was negligible; her manager, Larry Wanagas, reported that "somebody sent back one of her records, and that was it." And her mother remained untouched by "scandal." The *Advocate* interview was an emancipation, "like an emotional veil had been taken away," lang says. "I recommend it [coming out] to people who are ready to do it. Just do it."

lang displays her latest trophy, an MTV Award. Widely regarded as one of the best vocalists of her generation, the former country singer has achieved remarkable crossover success.

The times had swung in lang's favor. Within a year Melissa Etheridge and Elton John also came out publicly with no negative repercussions. Etheridge quipped that she was just "the Al Gore of lesbians," because lang's plunge had the greatest impact and made her own coming out easier. In the aftermath of her public admission, though, lang has been clear about her priorities, showing skepticism when lesbianism becomes the central focus of interviews. "Although I want to talk about it, like

I want to talk about my vegetarianism," she says, "I'm a singer—that's what I am foremost." While she says she is not interested in being cast as the "lesbian authority," lang recognizes the role she plays through her example and her music but doesn't believe that her contribution has been necessarily "political."

The gay film historian Vito Russo, who died of AIDS in 1990, would have interpreted lang's action differently. "Rock and pop stars," he wrote, "are international icons and role models, and to the degree that they reject traditional roles and gender imagery—for instance, iconoclastic k.d. lang and androgynous Boy George—they are social revolutionaries." lang's career had, in fact, been extremely political, and her coming-out was nothing short of historic.

Her sexual orientation was there all along, lang claims, for those who wanted to see it, and even for those who did not. As one of her recent interviewers put it, "It's hard to think of another woman who has so completely refused to conform to male-defined images of female sexuality."

"Elvis is alive—and she's beautiful!" Madonna said when she first met lang backstage at a concert. From the start of her career, k.d. lang's image was gender bending. She created for herself a powerfully nontraditional stage persona, a sort of butch and femme rolled into one who openly played with sexual ambiguity in dress and style and moved with a physical freedom uncommon to female performers. Early in her country career, she appeared to be dressing as both woman and man simultaneously, in full skirts with fringed cowboy shirts and cutoff men's boots. In later pop concerts, lang would start off in full butch drag, then, as the temperature on stage rose, slowly strip down to softer, more feminine clothing underneath.

In the early 1980s, performing songs written by men for men, lang turned them upside down and inside out. Her "Bopalena" video, a classic of lesbian camp, features lang in a kitschy Jackie Kennedy–style brocade suit and nylons, belting out the butch lyrics ("Bopalena, Bopalena, she's my gal/She's my gal and I love her so") with suggestively raised eyebrows. Later songs like "Big Big Love" were not as flagrant but were filled with double entendres about sexual arousal.

k. d. l a n g

And her crowd-pleasing "Big Boned Gal," still a hit at her concerts, celebrates a woman's pride in being exactly who she is, without having to please anyone, and testifies to a feminist consciousness that recurs—sometimes subtly and sometimes blatantly—throughout lang's music.

Certainly, country music, where lang first made her mark, had never seen anything like her before. In 1990, when lang won a Grammy for best female country vocalist, "I was watching the Grammys in a little hick bar," recalls the program director of a Wisconsin radio station, "and you could see the cross section of people. There was a couple . . . that cheered when lang won. But there were also two guys at the other end of the bar asking if that was a guy or a girl on screen."

It was not just her cropped hair or her choice of songs but also her assertive presence and manner that signaled lang's "difference." Female country stars were supposed to act demure and ladylike and to look more like Dolly Parton than Elvis Presley. And bad-girl rock stars like Madonna were the stuff heterosexual men's fantasies were made of. Where did k.d. lang fit in, with a performance style that was perceived as being more male than female?

"Men aren't used to women responding aggressively the way I do," lang told an interviewer in *Glamour* magazine in 1990. "Are we ready for a woman as strong and free as k.d.?" the magazine in turn asked its readers. And in a conversation with 1960s singer Lesley Gore in *Ms.* magazine that same year, lang spelled out her thoughts more clearly. "My personal fight," she told Gore, "is not to fall into the social formalization of what a woman should be. Although I don't necessarily hate an image like Dolly Parton's, because that's how she feels comfortable. I'm just saying . . . individuality in women is important. There's a strength there."

Reporters, reviewers, and interviewers everywhere referred to lang's "individuality" as "androgyny," but words like "oddball," "quirky," and "strange" also turned up in early newspaper and magazine features. Many articles on lang in the years before she came out, even the sympathetic ones, remarked on her physical appearance—particularly her haircut and her refusal to wear makeup—as an anomaly.

The press likened her not just to Elvis but to Ricky Nelson, Wayne Newton, a young John Lennon, Gene Autry, and Woody Wood-pecker—all males. "Tomboy," "boyish," and "masculine" were other overused descriptions of lang, code words that left little room for speculation.

After she came out and confirmed the rumors about her lesbianism, lang reflected that the term "androgyny" was simply a verbal trick that allowed the press to imply she was a lesbian without saying it overtly. Happily, lang had weathered the storm of public scrutiny and opinion and traveled a long route from her "tomboy" days in Alberta, Canada, to the point in time when she could openly use the "L word."

CHAPTER TWO

BIG BONED GAL

She was a big boned gal from southern Alberta.
You just couldn't call her small.

The girl who would become recording star k.d. lang hailed from the rugged Canadian province of Alberta, located just north of the state of Montana on the map. Alberta is best described as a land of contrasts, populated by diverse ethnic groups and distinguished by a range of geographic features—from the snowcapped Rocky Mountains and sparkling rivers of the west to the wide-open grassy plains of the central and southern regions. Like the western states just south of it, Alberta is a place where cowboys and ranchers staked their claims long ago, where beef remains king, and where "amber waves of grain" undulate in the wind. Like many Albertans, lang is a hardy product of the region's geography and an unusual blend of nationalities—Icelandic, Dutch, Sioux, English, Irish, Scottish, and German Jewish.

The youngest of four children, Kathryn Dawn Lang was born in Edmonton, the Albertan capital, on November 2, 1961. In the music world it was the year

At Consort High School Kathy Lang (seated, second from right) starred on the volleyball team, as well as in basketball, badminton, and track and field. Coach Larry Kjearsgaard (center) called her "a coach's dream."

the great country star Patsy Cline (a future k.d. lang icon) was finally making it big with "I Fall to Pieces," and Elvis was imploring, "Don't Be Cruel." Rocker Chubby Checker introduced a new dance phenomenon called "The Twist." Henry Mancini's easy-listening "Moon River," the theme from *Breakfast at Tiffany's*, prevailed at the Grammy Awards, and the film version of the musical *West Side Story* garnered an array of Oscars. And Roy Orbison's powerful "Crying," which k.d. lang would later record with great success, was climbing the charts.

From the beginning, everyone called her Kathy. She still refers to herself as Kathryn, not k.d., who is the performer, the celebrity, the star. "k.d. lang . . . is so much cooler than me," she confessed in *Rolling Stone* magazine.

Within a year after she was born, Kathy's parents moved her, her brother John, and sisters Jo Ann and Keltie southeast to Consort, a town of only 650 people, bounded by seemingly endless prairies. At distances of about 200 miles, Edmonton and Calgary were the nearest big cities, reached from Consort in those days on gravel roads. Surrounded by a landscape of grain fields and elevators, cattle-grazing pastures, and oil rigs, lang's hometown had "one TV channel, one radio station, no movie theaters, one bar, one drugstore, no police—and no swimming pool," lang recalled in *Vanity Fair* magazine. The closest movie theater was 30 miles away in Coronation. Off Consort's main drag, called 50th Street, there was just a scattering of side streets, with no pavement until the early 1970s. The Langs lived in a one-story bungalow on the edge of town, with nothing but fields and blue sky on one side of it. The cover for k.d. lang's third album, *Absolute Torch and Twang*, was photographed in the area, showing the singer adrift in golden wheat, with billowing clouds dotting the limitless horizon. As a child, she loved the geography of the region and still speaks fondly of "the wind, the openness."

Today, lang muses about the benefits of growing up in such a small town, which might sound to many like a stifling experience. On the contrary, lang believes it helped fuel her imagination and creativity. "Growing up in Consort, you took what you could get," she told *Vanity Fair,* "and you found something positive and creative in everything.

Audrey Lang, a soft-spoken second-grade teacher, encouraged her daughter to express herself through music, driving more than 100 miles round-trip each week to take Kathy to her piano and singing lessons.

Every sort of information I got would be a huge thing for my fantasy life. An album cover would be like a movie—a whole other dimension I would travel in, like stepping through the looking glass." The "mediocrity" of her hometown is something lang feels she has embraced and incorporated into her art—especially in her early career, when kitsch figured prominently in her work "Small-town things are part of what I am," she believes "You know, old guys playing music at dances and bake sales." Also, in a town the size of Consort, everyone gets to know their neighbors intimately, "so their eccentricities seem normal," lang muses. "I never thought to curb my own eccentricity."

Fred Lang, Kathy's father, owned and operated the Consort drug-store, while Audrey Lang, her mother, taught second grade in the local elementary school. "We had a pretty normal family," lang remembers. "We had supper every night at six o'clock, and Saturday morning I had to vacuum the carpet and clean the bathrooms."

But unlike many other parents, lang's mother and father raised her relatively free of gender stereotypes. lang has fond memories of her mother telling her she was "handsome" when she was young. "I really loved that she said 'handsome,'" she told the *Advocate,* "because . . . that's breaking stereotypes. You're very handsome, and you don't need to wear makeup."

In many ways, "My parents brought me up with no limitations," lang has reflected. "They supported my self-confidence and never said, 'Only boys can do that.'" Indeed, young Kathy engaged in many activities that were the traditional realm of boys. Her father dubbed her his "boy-girl" and bought her a motorcycle when she was nine, a Yamaha 60 Mini-Enduro, making her the only girl in Consort to own one. It was the first in a long line of bikes, down to the custom Harley Springer she rides today. "Every year I would take that thing apart and clean it and put it back together," she recently recalled; but the most fun was thundering through town, imagining she was Starsky or Hutch from the popular TV series. "I like the romance of being on a motorcycle," lang says. "I love the wind . . . the aloneness."

Father and daughter used to go shooting together, and Kathy had her own shotgun when she was only 12. "I was a marksman," lang remembers, but she never took aim at animals, only targets. Kathy and Fred "would lie down at the front of the family drugstore," reporter Don Gillmor detailed in *Saturday Night* magazine, "and shoot through to a target in the dispensary at the back. They went to shooting matches together, and Kathy often returned with prizes."

Her earliest ambition was to be a Roller Derby queen. She and Keltie would watch roller derby on TV—"It was the only thing that came on TV on Saturday," lang remembers, "that was worth watching." lang later joked with talk-show host Jay Leno, "There was a time I was headed straight for the Canadian Thunderbirds. Amazons on wheels. Very exciting."

lang reflects that her tomboy recreations gave her "the self-confidence which few girls have the advantage of." She felt comfortable not only with traditionally "male" activities but also with traditionally "male" attractions and desires. lang says now that she knew she was a lesbian at an early age—in fact, before she'd ever heard the word. She recounts a story about playing Batman and Robin with two little boys when she was five. At one point in the game they were all going home to their spouses. The boys announced that "they were going home to their wives. I said I was going home to my wife, too. They said, 'You can't have a wife.' I said, 'Yes, I can.' . . . My earliest memories are of being attracted to women." Like many young lesbians, Kathy developed crushes on female teachers, and she remembers that "whenever an intelligent, strong woman came to town who looked independent and who had gone to study at university and had traveled around, it was like, 'I want to get to know you.'"

Both of her parents fostered her early interest in music. Audrey Lang purchased a used piano in Edmonton, making monthly payments on it from her household account. When Kathy was seven, she, John, and their mother began driving once a week to Castor, about 60 miles west of Consort on Highway 12, so that the children could have piano lessons with Sister Xavier at the Theresetta Convent. Even in the foulest weather (and Alberta winters can be brutal), they arrived on time, and Kathy grew restless in the convent waiting room while John took his lesson first. Listening to him do his scales over and over, lang believes, was one thing that helped her develop her ear for music. lang avows that from that time on she was in love with music. "I knew what I wanted to be the day I had my first piano lesson."

A strict disciplinarian, Sister Xavier "was the one who got me into singing," lang says now. During the first year of lessons, Sister Xavier asked if Kathy would like to sing at a music festival in Coronation. "She had a pretty voice even then," Sister Xavier recalled later, and "wonderful breath control." The child's answer was simple and earnest, the response of someone who, even at a young age, imagined celebrity for herself. "Oh, could I?" she asked. From then on, Kathy sang at local festivals, school functions, weddings, and competitions, which she usually won.

In *Ms.* magazine, lang reminisced with Lesley Gore about how she practiced singing at home "in front of the full-length mirror. . . . I wanted an audience all the time." In fact, Audrey Lang dates her daughter's flair for entertainment to "the age of two," she told Don Gillmor. "She always got the spotlight. She had boundless energy." Songwriting partner Ben Mink has called lang "a born ham. There's

k. d. lang

Anne Murray, Canada's most successful pop singer in the 1970s, provided a role model for young Kathy. Years later, lang would sing a duet of "I Want To Sing You a Love Song" with her childhood idol on a Canadian television country music special.

some famous footage of her at her first or second birthday party, and you can see the charisma. She was always an entertainer."

"Everybody knew what my dream was," lang remembers, but the family didn't dwell on Kathy's musical ambition. "The only thing my mum ever said was, 'If you're going to be onstage, you're going to need braces.' And I'm glad I got them, because I feel much more confident now."

Kathy grew up with an eclectic appreciation for music. The Langs had an old record player and an assortment of albums, from Broadway musicals and movie soundtracks to Chubby Checker and Percy Faith.

Early favorites of Kathy's were *Doctor Zhivago, My Fair Lady, South Pacific, Oklahoma!,* and *The Sound of Music,* and she had a "thing," she recalls, for Julie Andrews. "My first hero was Maria [von Trapp]."

Though country music wasn't popular with her and her siblings, lang remembers that one of her favorite TV shows was "The Beverly Hillbillies," whose rousing theme song was played on banjo and guitar by bluegrass masters Lester Flatt and Earl Scruggs. The Clampetts "influenced me a lot," lang says; "they were so honest compared to their surroundings." lang also remembers being a fan of Anne Murray, the Canadian country star, who was the first vocalist young Kathy ever saw in concert. "When I was nine," lang told *Musician* magazine, "I wrote her a song. I think it was called 'Let's Try It Together.' It was a 'We Are the World'–type song." Writing in purple magic marker, Kathy sent the song off to Murray with her permission "to write music to these lyrics," but she never got a reply. lang still respects Murray as "one of the only Canadian performers to retain her citizenship and her identity as a Canadian."

As Kathy got older, she and her sister Keltie became devoted to Joe Cocker, Maria Muldaur, Creedence Clearwater Revival, Leon Russell, and the Allman Brothers—all rock 'n' rollers—and her changing interests in music coincided with giving up classical piano lessons at about age 10. Kathy had become frustrated with daily practice and felt constrained by following the notes as they were written on the page. Not surprisingly, Kathy got her first guitar soon after she quit her piano lessons. lang has told a variety of contradictory stories over the years about when and where she got the guitar. Most recently, she reported that it was her father who bought her an electric guitar for Christmas in about sixth grade.

Though the early years for Kathy Lang were pretty routine, her world turned upside down the year she was 12. That year, her father took off, abandoning his wife and children for another woman. "When he left, he left," Audrey Lang says. "I don't know where he lives, I truly don't. I don't think any of the kids know either."

The sudden and complete departure of her father, to whom she had been very close, threw Kathy into shock. "It was very sudden and drastic," lang told *Vanity Fair* years later. "I didn't hear from him for about eight years, until I ran into him on the street in Edmonton one time." lang's manager, Larry Wanagas, recalls that Fred Lang also showed up at one of his daughter's concerts and watched with tears streaming down his face.

"My father was a very charming man in public," Keltie Lang remembers, "and we liked him because he bought us stuff. But, at home, he wasn't really there, from that whole generation of absentee dads who were absentee even though they were sitting at the dinner table."

lang admits now that she knew there was trouble between her parents, but it was the way her father vanished that was so upsetting. It was hard for her, she says, to see her mother going through such an ordeal. "My mother would teach in the day and go down and try to run the store. I had to take on some of the responsibilities, whether it was working in the drugstore or getting home on time so my mother wouldn't worry. I went from being a kid to being an adult very fast."

"I just think [my father] felt like he couldn't deal with what was happening in his own life," lang rationalizes. But she traces her own difficulty with maintaining intimate relationships in adulthood to the continuing effects of his leaving—"a deep pool of pain," she has called it. "There is a difficulty trusting," she disclosed to *Vanity Fair*. "I think I sabotage relationships because I'm afraid of being left again." But she insists that she no longer feels angry about his departure. "A wound is just a highway to a new and enlightened kind of confidence," she has philosophized. "Damage is one of the things in emotional aesthetics that makes something great, like all the scars on a tree or a banged–up coffee cup or whatever."

Because Keltie, her closest sibling in age, was five years older and off at college, Kathy's teenage years were spent alone with her mother. They built a strong relationship that has lasted to the present, and lang professes that she has always adored her mother. It was their close and loving bond that enabled Kathy, at age 17, to reveal her sexual orientation to her mother. "I didn't want to live a life of dishonesty with my mother," lang relates. "I wanted her to understand me. And I had known this for years and years and years."

Though considered unconventional by some, Kathy was a fairly typical high school student—popular, busy with sports and extra-curricular activities, and eager to find adventures beyond her small hometown.

Happily, her mother took the news well. She must not have been too surprised, given that her tomboy daughter didn't care to date boys and had already developed a butch style that included wearing suits and ties, even in a high school yearbook photograph. Though she wore a dress to her senior prom, Kathy completed the outfit with a pair of hiking boots.

Besides her attraction to girls—"anyone I could get my hands on, basically," lang quips now—Kathy's two overriding interests, music and sports, were the themes of her young adult years. Accompanying herself on guitar, she continued to sing at socials and weddings throughout high school, her repertoire including songs such as "Silver Threads and Golden Needles" and "The First Time Ever I Saw Your Face." At the age of 14, she composed her first complete song, "Hoping My Dreams Come True," while on a girls' basketball trip to Halifax, Nova Scotia.

Indeed, she was famous for singing on the court during games and in the bus on team road trips. Volleyball coach Larry Kjearsgaard, who drove the bus, recollects that "those trips were never dull. I'll always remember Kathy sitting in the back of the bus belting out 'That'll Be the Day.'" On the way home from one school trip, Kathy charmed Kjearsgaard into making a detour, because she was registered in the Coronation Music Festival that day and had forgotten to mention it. Wearing a bright yellow track suit over her volleyball uniform, she "just walked in, . . . sang, won, and left."

In 1977 Kathy had her first paid performance at Las Vegas Casino Night at the Consort Kinsmen Club. Playing her 12-string guitar, she sang three songs and earned $25. About that time, she began signing her name "Kathy Lang" with a star after it, because she believed she was headed for celebrity. In a letter to her sister Keltie at college, Kathy wrote, "Keep this, because the signature will be worth something one day."

Music always won out over studying. "Even though my mother was a teacher, I was a terrible student," lang confesses. "I never studied.

In her senior year at Consort High, Kathy served as editor of the school yearbook and posed for a photograph in that capacity wearing a man's suit and tie. At this time, she also self-confidently added a flourish to her signature: a star to symbolize her future celebrity.

I just figured, what's the use? I always knew that it would be like it is now, that I'd be making records and doing concerts, so it made no sense for me to study algebra."

Kathy composed and performed her high school graduation theme song, "The End of Our Beginning," and in the 1979 high school yearbook, for which she was the editor, announced that she was "headed for a career in music." This was despite the fact that she had taken an aptitude test that said she was "98 percent guaranteed to become a mechanic," lang notes with amusement. In fact, many who knew her at Consort High assumed that if she did achieve fame it would be as an athlete, possibly at the Olympic level, rather than as a musician.

Sports were her other consuming passion, and Kathy was a girl jock who excelled at everything she tried. "I played absolutely every sport," lang states. "I lived for sports. Especially volleyball. When you live in a small town and you're not a boy and don't play hockey, there's not much else to do." Besides being a star on the girls' volleyball team, Kathy also played girls' basketball and competed in various track-and-field events. In 12th grade she ranked eighth in Canada in the javelin throw. Consort High School named her Athlete of the Year three years in a row.

Sports may have also helped strengthen her body image, tarnished in adolescence by jokes about her large frame. Tall and broad, Kathy Lang was definitely a "big boned gal." "I was 170 pounds in the seventh grade," lang says. "My brother and sister used to call me 'Mama Kath Elliot,' so I was scarred for life." "She was a big girl, and very strong," one of her coaches remembers, noting that what Kathy lacked in coordination she made up in simple strength—of body and of will.

"Now a chance to find the dreams/Breaking out of dependent seams," were the closing words of Kathy's song "The End of Our Beginning." Given her interests and determination to succeed, it was no wonder that Kathy chose to pursue her dreams at Red Deer College, which boasted both a well-known volleyball team and a solid music department. As sister Keltie observed, "She just picks a destiny and works toward it."

CHAPTER THREE

DRIFTING

"I just knew when it was time to leave I was going to leave," k.d. lang says, referring to her hometown of Consort. "My dreams didn't have anything to do with staying there."

After a summer of driving a three ton grain truck to earn extra money, Kathy Lang and her dreams headed west to college, to the city of Red Deer in central Alberta. Just a two-hour drive from home, Red Deer promised more cultural opportunities and stimulation than Consort, and Red Deer College offered Kathy the chance to study music and voice while participating in team athletics.

One of the first things Kathy did after signing up for a full load of classes was to try out for the women's volleyball team. Surprisingly, even with a letter of recommendation from her high school coach, she didn't make the cut. One story has it that the college coach didn't appreciate her attitude or her eccentricities, particularly the way she liked to sing on the court in the middle of play. But Larry Kjearsgaard, her high school volleyball coach, remembers that Kathy

As a college student, Lang appears confidently ready to take on the world. Early in her college days she decided to focus her energies on a career in music.

elaborated to him on why she did not make the team. "Practices were five days a week," he told lang biographer Victoria Starr, "and one of her music classes—I believe it was a voice class—overlapped with practice on one of those days. So she asked permission to miss half of practice this one day a week, and the coach basically told her no, she would have to choose." In Kathy's mind there was no choice.

Soon Kathy began to devote all of her time and energy to music, and this provoked a clash with her mother. Like many parents whose children aspire to careers in the arts, Audrey worried that her daughter was chasing a pipe dream when she should have been preparing herself for a "real" job, like teaching physical education. Kathy, on her first visit home from college, accused Audrey of hampering her. "Why did you let me quit piano lessons?" she confronted her mother.

lang recalls that she was soon restless in college and "unhappy with the narrow academic requirements." Biographer Victoria Starr relates that while college classes helped Kathy with certain technical aspects of singing—she discovered there, for example, that she was a mezzo-soprano—the formal academic structure frustrated her. Her disappointment with college harks back to her childhood impatience with classical piano lessons. "They oppressed our creativity," lang has said of her college music teachers. "If it couldn't be written down, they wouldn't accept it. They just didn't get it."

Biographer William Robertson has speculated that in Consort Kathy was accustomed to acting eccentric and getting attention—whether tooling around town on her motorcycle at 9, or dressing in patched leather pants with a headband at 11, or singing out loud on the high school basketball court. But it was more difficult to express herself freely in the college classroom, where study was formalized and there was no apparent interest in the avant-garde.

Kathy quickly found an alternative way to nurture her independent spirit through a group of supportive and like-minded friends who were also music and art students. Her closest companion was Gary Elgar, whom everyone called Drifter. He had come west from Ontario to work in the oil fields and ended up taking music classes at Red Deer, where he met Kathy. They soon discovered shared interests in music and poetry. Drifter was, in lang's memory, "very much like John Lennon," and she describes their platonic friendship as nothing short of spiritual. "We were the same person in different bodies, we were that close," she says reverently.

Years after her untimely death, country legend Patsy Cline continues to inspire listeners. The spirited singer's recordings touched something deep within lang, who came to believe that "somehow I've inherited her emotions, her soul."

k. d. lang

Drifter and his "anything goes" philosophy about creating art had an enormous influence on Kathy, who was open to trying and doing everything. Together they were "experimenting with noise," as lang puts it, using Drifter's reel-to-reel tape recorder to splice together bits of conversations, sounds of banging kitchen utensils, and boisterous jam sessions on instruments they barely knew how to play. Richard Houghton, one of Kathy and Drifter's friends from those days, described their approach to art to Victoria Starr as "whatever you did, if it was honest, it was acceptable."

Over the next year, Kathy, Drifter, and their troupe experimented with a range of performance and conceptual art. "We took it very seriously," lang says. After Barney Clarke underwent his famous heart transplant surgery, Kathy and her friends decided to stage a reenactment of it. "We moved into an art gallery, set up an 'operating theater,' and mimed doing surgery for twelve hours," lang recalls with amusement. The "heart" was, in fact, made of pickled vegetables. One performance piece involved crawling around onstage in garbage bags, à la Lennon and Ono. At another time, with $500 worth of helium balloons, they created a "sky sculpture" of a 36-foot man.

"Performance art," lang muses now, "is all about seeing the different dimensions of a subject and conglomerating all your emotional responses without making a conclusive statement." It was well suited to her personality, and, she says, "a natural step" from there to the country music she began performing not long after.

lang has described those days in Red Deer as "sort of like being a beatnik. There was poetry reading and music twenty-four hours a day. I was living what I thought I had missed by missing the sixties." It was during that time in Red Deer that she also began to practice vegetarianism, though her brother John had kindled the flame of it in her when she was a child. "It was always in me," she says now. Consort, however, was in the heart of cattle country, and "it would have been a little tough to grow up where I did and say, 'Mom, don't cook animals.'" She dates the official day of her liberation from meat eating to January 3, 1981, though she did not completely stop wearing leather until 10 years later.

After three semesters of college, Kathy decided to drop out to follow her own creative pursuits full-time, unhampered by the restrictions of teachers and classes. But instead of working on a performance career, she seemed to concentrate more on hanging out—listening to Joni Mitchell, Linda Ronstadt, and Rickie Lee Jones records, drinking beer with her friends and experimenting with hashish, and working dead-end jobs in between frequent road trips with Drifter and Houghton. On one cross-country trip to Toronto, Drifter unexpectedly announced that he would not be returning to Red Deer but intended to stay with his family in the east for a while. "When he went back to Ontario, I could see she really, really missed him," Audrey Lang says, remembering her daughter's reaction to the loss of Drifter. "She almost grieved to have him back."

On her own without her spiritual other half, Kathy decided in 1981 to move to Edmonton, where she had spent a lot of time over the last few years. She wanted to accomplish finally what she had set out to do when she left Consort—establish a career in music. But it also must have been important to her, as a young lesbian, to be part of a larger gay community, and she quickly found a circle of friends with whom she often went to the gay disco and a girlfriend who supported her for a while so she could sing, play the guitar, and paint.

During this time, Kathy determinedly pushed on with her career, handing out business cards with "Kathy Lang, Vocalist" on them and hoping for someone to recognize and reward her talent. lang says she secured her first appearance in Edmonton by approaching local country singer Holly Wright in a hotel parking lot and requesting an "impromptu audition." Amazingly, after hearing her sing, Wright invited Kathy to open for her at the Alberta Provincial Archives Museum on November 13, 1981—just days after Kathy's 20th birthday.

Kathy's second, more significant break cropped up not long after, when she was on one of her frequent trips back to Red Deer that fall. Doug Newell, who was teaching in the drama department at Red Deer College, heard her sing and play guitar at a party. He was coproducing a play in Edmonton called *Country Chorale,* in which the main character, Ruby, dreams of being a country music star but gets

Lang and her soul mate, Gary Elgar, who was known as Drifter, prepare to embark on a cross-country trip to Toronto. Their friend Richard Houghton remembers, "Put them together and the cliché is Lennon and McCartney, but it was kind of like that. Together they were more than the sum of their parts."

sidetracked by marriage, work, and pregnancy. Her only relief from her tedious life is listening to a radio program called "Country Chorale." Four actors standing to the side of the stage represent the voices of the women Ruby hears singing.

Newell knew that the play's director was searching for an actor to take the role of the fourth woman, and he thought Kathy could handle the part. He called the director, Stephen Heatley, who in turn called Kathy and offered her the job. It was unpaid, but Kathy saw it as a chance for exposure and eagerly accepted the role, though she knew very little about country music and was not even sure she liked it.

Ray Storey, who wrote *Country Chorale*'s lyrics and dialogue, envisioned June Ritter, the character Kathy was portraying, as a singer in the style of the celebrated country artist Patsy Cline. "Who's Patsy Cline?" Kathy reportedly inquired. In the early 1980s it was not an unusual question for a young person not raised on country music. Cline had died in a plane crash in 1963 after recording only a handful of hit records; though her voice and style were legendary in Nashville, kids like Kathy Lang, who grew up in the 1970s listening to rock 'n' roll, were unlikely to have heard of her.

Patsy Cline enjoyed a short but brilliant career. Like k.d. lang, she was promoting herself and searching for a hit song for years before she ever became successful, and was finally propelled to the top of both the country and pop charts by her now-classic "I Fall to Pieces." In the 18 months that followed, before her death at age 30, she recorded such timeless favorites as "She's Got You," "Crazy," and "Sweet Dreams (of You)." "She was a great singer, a belter," country artist Roger Miller said of her sound, a combination of a powerful voice and an extraordinary range that wrapped around a song and exposed its emotional core. The improvised growls, trills, and jubilant yodels that she incorporated into her work are famous. Cline was the first female country star to cross over into pop, though she always resisted performing any song that she felt was not country enough, but what she called just "a little ole pop song."

Guided by innovative producer Owen Bradley, Cline's unique style was an important part of a "new Nashville sound," which piloted country music beyond its "hillbilly" past and helped it compete with rock 'n' roll. But the ramifications of her role in the country music arena were even greater. Patsy Cline was a strong, outspoken, and openly sexual woman in an industry that had always preferred women to be window dressing. "Her massive appeal," her friend, country star Dottie West, has written, "proved women, without men by their side, could consistently sell records and draw audiences." Cline's example would have a profound influence on a whole generation of female country singers, which included such performers as Loretta Lynn, Brenda Lee, and Dottie West herself. Cline's biographer, Ellis Nassour, states emphatically that she "changed the entire perception of women in country music."

To help Kathy get into the Patsy Cline character for *Country Chorale,* Ray Storey reportedly showed Kathy one of Cline's album covers, with the country star in a sassy pose, hands on her hips and a forthright look in her eyes. Kathy worked on imitating the pose and soon had it down pat. "Sometimes you give a performer one thing that becomes the key that unlocks the door," *Chorale* director Stephen Heatley has said of Kathy's appropriation of Cline's stance.

Then, to aid her preparation for the role, Storey gave Kathy her first Patsy Cline record. "I remember the night I got that record," recalls lang, "playing 'I Wish I Didn't Love You So' and feeling all the emotions that song brought out in me. It just seemed to turn the sky purple and make the moon full. I thought, 'This is what I've gotta do.'"

Kathy heard more in Patsy Cline's work than she had thought country music had to offer. "I heard jazz, rockabilly, and blues all incorporated into country music. It was like she [Patsy] came knocking at my door and I acknowledged her." When she listened to Patsy for the first time, "everything went 'click.'"

Country Chorale opened in March of 1982 in Red Deer, then moved on to Edmonton for a short run. Reviewers favored the play, and some cited Kathy Lang's performance as June Ritter as particularly memorable. But despite the good reviews and her engaging imitation of Cline, Kathy was cut from the cast of *Country Chorale* when the producers decided to take it on tour across Canada later that year. Director Heatley

Although Red Deer College presented Lang with the opportunity to study singing's technical aspects and meet interesting new people, she quickly found the academic environment creatively stifling.

had to pare down the cast for touring, and Kathy would have had to play one additional part, that of a shy, airheaded girl. It wasn't a role that she took to naturally, as she had to the brassy Patsy Cline character; in fact, her singing talent proved much stronger than her acting skills.

The cut might have been a setback for another performer, but Kathy had already announced to the *Chorale* cast that she expected to be famous. Dismissing her claims as youthful arrogance, her colleagues found to their amazement that by the time they had returned from their cross-Canada tour everyone in Edmonton seemed to be talking about a singer named k.d. lang.

CHAPTER FOUR

SAY HI TO PATSY FOR ME

After *Country Chorale* set off to tour Canada without her, Kathy Lang noticed an advertisement in an Edmonton newspaper that would change her life. Dance Party, a western swing band, needed a female vocalist and had booked audition time at the Edmonton recording studio of Lars ("Larry") Wanagas, who also managed some local bands. Wanagas later described Kathy Lang's audition at his studio, Homestead Recorders, to *Alberta Report:* "She just sang some straightforward country songs, Emmylou Harris and Patsy Cline, but she sang them exceptionally well. It was obvious she had a lot of talent."

The members of Dance Party were equally impressed and hired her on the spot, but, unfortunately, the group disbanded after only one performance. Another setback for Lang was promptly turned around, this time by Larry Wanagas, who landed her some radio commercials for local stores. But both of them knew that she could achieve much more. By

Newly christened k.d. lang (in lowercase letters in homage to poet e.e. cummings), the country singer fashioned an extremely unconventional stage persona with her short, spiky hair, ripped stockings, sawed-off cowboy boots, and campy costumes.

mid-1983 the two had struck a deal for Wanagas to manage her career, which he has done ever since. "I haven't let her out of my sight," he says.

The question was what style of music was best suited for her powerful voice and range. Later, lang claimed that it was the influence of Patsy Cline that pulled her image together for her. "I got out the Cline records and it just went click," she said. "I saw myself, how I was going to dress, how I was going to move. I saw the kind of singing I was going to do, saw how my band was going to sound."

lang's choice of country music, however, was probably a more practical one than that. "When she first came to me," Wanagas has said, "she said she wanted to be a jazz singer. I said if you want to be a jazz singer the first thing to do is build yourself a little platform so that once you have some notoriety and success, you have a lot easier time with it. If we start pushing you as a jazz singer at twenty years old, we're all going to starve." Since country music was popular in Edmonton clubs, and lang had already successfully tried her hand at it in *Country Chorale,* it seemed like a logical choice for her. Wanagas helped her pick a few songs, hire a band, and get some gigs around town. By late 1983, she was hitting the clubs of Edmonton as k.d. lang.

k.d. lang was a "unique creation," as one magazine put it. The performer that the Edmonton music scene was talking about in late 1983 and early 1984 shopped for her costumes at local thrift stores and appeared on stage in full skirts with plastic cowboys and Indians sewn up the side, western blouses, and worn cowboy boots cut off at the ankles. From the beginning, she shaped her own legend, telling audiences that the boots were a gift from a Polish-Ukrainian farmer, which she cut off so they could be worn with narrow-leg pants. "Then I realized how cool they looked," she smiled. Topping off the outfit was a pair of metal-framed glasses without lenses. "I just liked them," she explained about the seemingly useless prop. "They make me feel stately, like my mom. But they're so ugly. . . . They help lower my self-esteem on stage, and I think that makes me more accessible."

Wearing these kitschy costumes, Kathy Lang created a character who was quickly described in the press as "mad" and "oddball." Urging all the "Bobs and Bettys" in the audience to have a "wing-ding daddy-o of a good time," stage persona k.d. lang performed with what would later be called "almost cartoonish freneticism," writhing on the floor to the song "Johnny Get Angry" or strutting her stuff to "These Boots Are Made for Walkin'." Her antics were the talk of Edmonton; people began to jam clubs like the Sidetrack Cafe to see what all the fuss was about, and if she really wore stockings with holes in them on purpose.

Beyond stirring up a sensation, lang couldn't really describe at that time where her performance style was headed. "There's a long-term concept around k.d. lang," she told one reporter, "but I can't tell you exactly how it goes because it's very difficult to put concepts into words. . . . Sure, it's corny, but I think people are beginning to get smart enough to realize that most emotions are corny, that corny is real life."

Clearly, it had been just a short step from her performance art past. Her first fans in the Edmonton clubs tended to be devotees of alternative music, who liked the humor she incorporated into her performances, but lang also wanted to reach traditional country music fans. "It's like a ladder," she said, describing what she hoped would be the appeal of her style, "where some people can reach the top: the real bizarros. And the very straight people can catch onto the bottom rung, and just cry into their beer to 'I Fall to Pieces.'"

At this point in her new career, lang's admiration of Patsy Cline took a puzzling turn, which added to her eccentric image. Inspiration is something people can readily understand, but lang started to allege that she was not just inspired by Cline, she was, in fact, her reincarnation. "She began to recall a dimly remembered dream that recurred throughout her childhood; a plane, a storm outside, and a fiery crash," wrote one reporter. "The more I believed it," lang said, "the more I felt it, and the more I felt free enough to believe it." She even named her new band the reclines in honor of the connection to Patsy.

There were many skeptics who contended that talking about reincarnation was just a clever way for the aspiring star to draw more attention to herself. "I am tired of people thinking it's a put-on," lang later told the *Toronto Star.* "Somehow I've inherited her emotions, her soul. . . . I have a recurring dream about a plane crash . . . and others where I

Ultrafeminine Dolly Parton epitomizes the traditional image of a female country star. Although strong, independent women have always been a part of country music, they have become much more visible lately with the success of lang, Mary Chapin Carpenter, Roseanne Cash, and others.

actually have conversations with her [Patsy]." lang continued to speak of their spiritual connection with great fervor for years to come, though she would eventually tone down the boldness of the "reincarnation" statement: "I believe I have a very strong tie to Patsy because when I hear her music or sing her music, I can absorb it so easily and so completely."

In the spring of 1984, Wanagas thought it was time for k.d. lang to record her first single, "Friday Dance Promenade," "a sashaying honky-tonker," as biographer William Robertson put it, written by lang and splashed with references to Patsy Cline. On the flip side of the record was "Damned Old Dog," a seventies tune originally written and performed by the Roches, a New York band. The seven-inch single was pressed on white vinyl and is now a collector's item.

lang's popularity in the local clubs made it possible for Wanagas to get her a booking on the Canadian country music television show "Sun Country," and a magazine interview in the weekly *Alberta Report*. "Sun

Country" was lang's initiation into the straitlaced world of country music, which expected a certain look for its performers and would, over the years, often criticize her nonconformity. Country "girl singers" were supposed to follow the look of the great Nashville Sound artists like Patsy Cline, Loretta Lynn, and Tammy Wynette, wearing sparkling gowns and their hair teased and curled high on their heads. lang would later say that the unwritten rule in country music was "the higher the hair, the closer to God."

But that look didn't suit k.d. lang. Her campy western wear was country-with-humor, but not everyone at "Sun Country" got the joke. "First my boots were condemned," she subsequently told *Alberta Report* about her first TV experience. "Then they came at me with a curling iron, saying they wanted to take the 'edge' off my hair." Toned down by a sedate black dress with sparkling rhinestone buttons and a pair of conventional white western boots, lang performed a coolly sassy version of "Friday Dance Promenade" as Kathy Lang, revealing none of the madcap frenzy of the club performer k.d. lang. She was clearly adjusting her image to please the traditional country music audience that regularly watched "Sun Country," and she explained her acquiescence in *Alberta Report:* "I'll be anything they want me to be. . . . But then I'll turn around and be a thousand other things beside."

Within no time, k.d. lang and the reclines were commanding bookings in small clubs and on college campuses all over Alberta, with each show drawing a sellout crowd and bringing in more money and notoriety for lang. At one of these gigs in the town of Jasper in the Rockies in April 1984, lang learned just before she went on stage that her friend Drifter had been savagely killed while trying to stop a party brawl in Red Deer, where he had recently returned. Shocked and upset, lang decided not to cancel the engagement, but went on and gave the performance her all. "I got up there and sang my guts out," she told *Alberta Report.* "I couldn't understand why he'd been murdered." Later, she spent the night walking through the mountains alone, mourning her soul mate.

For weeks, lang was shaken by her friend's murder and dreamed about him repeatedly, once even seeing him in her room in the middle of the night. She talked about him very little but kept him quietly in her heart. "My spiritual side was always awake, but since Drifter's death it has been strong," she said later that year. "He helped me. My music career has moved faster than any I can think of, and it's Drifter and Patsy who are doing it."

Just a month after Drifter's death, k.d. lang and the reclines recorded their first album at Larry Wanagas's Homestead Recorders studio. Though the band was earning decent money, lang had to borrow from her mother to help finance the costly project, and Wanagas contributed studio time. Produced by the newly created Bumstead Records, the album, called *A Truly Western Experience,* consisted of nine songs lang and the band had been playing at their club gigs, five of which— including "Pine and Stew" and "Hanky Panky"—had been written by her and members of the band. Others, like "There You Go" and "Stop, Look, and Listen," had previously been recorded by Patsy Cline. "Bopalena," written by Webb Pierce and Mel Tillis of Nashville fame, was clearly meant for a man to sing, but lang made it her own.

The final track on the album had been written by Drifter and was called "Hooked On Junk." Not a country song by any stretch of the imagination, "Hooked On Junk" resembled the most avant-garde (and hard to sell) music of John Lennon and Yoko Ono and was the final vestige of lang's performance art past. Determined to honor her friend even if she drew negative reviews for the album, lang told *Alberta Report* that she had included the out-of-place song "for Drifter. He wrote it. That's why I put it on the record."

The album's cover design was lang's creation, a cut-and-paste farm scene of lang walking a fence to a barn, where a photo of Patsy Cline appears in the loft. Below the song titles and credits on the back cover lang included the line, "and the wind drifts through my soul, say hi to patsy for me"—a tribute to Drifter and Patsy Cline, her two spiritual mentors.

The album appeared on the day before a performance that would be a turning point for lang and her band. On August 10, 1984, k.d. lang and the reclines had a choice gig at the annual Edmonton Folk Festival before a crowd of several thousand, including a healthy pinch of record executives and agents. The band scheduled to follow the reclines that Friday night got lost on the way to the festival, and lang and her band got to play for 40 minutes instead of just 20. Fired up and ready to make the most of her good fortune, lang managed to bring the house down.

"She was the best thing that happened all weekend," said Richard Flohil, a Toronto publicist, of lang's performance. "She had ten times more energy than anyone else who hit the stage and her act was unlike anything I'd ever seen." The *Edmonton Sun* reported the next day that lang "roared around the stage like a riderless motorcycle." That night, lang received her first standing ovation, for a powerful a cappella rendition of "Amazing Grace," which she saved for her closing number. As an encore, she delivered a heartfelt version of Patsy Cline's "I Fall to Pieces."

"I'm gonna swagger, and I'm gonna have fun up here, and I'm gonna be sexy, and I don't have to look like Dolly Parton to do it," asserted lang, responding iconoclastically to Nashville's expectations of women.

k.d. lang

Flohil headed back to Toronto to spread the word about lang, who he realized was the hottest thing to hit the Canadian music scene in his career. But he found that the news about k.d. lang and the reclines had radiated on its own, brought back east by musicians and handlers who had witnessed the amazing performance in Edmonton. Selling the band in Toronto would be easy. With Flohil striking a deal with Wanagas to promote the event, k.d. lang and the reclines were booked for their eastern debut, at a Toronto bar called Albert's Hall.

In the meantime, thanks to fans who had seen lang perform, *A Truly Western Experience* sold out its initial run of 1,000 copies, and by October there was a second pressing of 1,000. By the time the band got to their Toronto engagement in late October 1984, people were lining up to see the amazing k.d. lang and the reclines at the intimate club that held

lang romps with her guitar, exhibiting characteristic energy and humor. Her powerful voice and oddball onstage antics quickly attracted sell-out crowds and music industry attention.

about 150 people. "There was a line-up on a Monday night," said Flohil, who had worked hard to publicize the event. "I don't think I've ever seen a line-up on a Monday night in Toronto. She got incredible attention there." With so much ballyhoo, Flohil and Wanagas hoped that the Albert's Hall performance would either generate or at least pave the way for a recording contract for lang.

By midweek, *Toronto Globe and Mail* reporter Liam Lacey was writing that lang had turned Toronto "on its collective ear." He described the stage antics that had made her so popular in Alberta: "[She] runs about the stage, into washrooms and out doorways as she sings." But Lacey, like many others, saw behind the frenzied exterior. "Lang's live show is an exultant experience," he praised, as he proclaimed her "a first-rate country singer with a warm, vibrant, and heart-rending voice."

But even with lang's great reviews and sold-out performances, her handlers were having trouble stirring up any interest among record companies, who did not know what to make of the singer's unusual, flamboyant style. Her music did not fit into the neat categories that the record companies were accustomed to. What, they wondered, was the market for the hybrid k.d. lang and the reclines? *Canadian Composer* quoted one record company executive's fear that the band "might fall into the gulf . . . between rock and country."

Indeed, radio stations—also stringent about categories—were confused by her sound. As one program director at an Edmonton country station put it, "K. D. Lang is a little too borderline . . . her image is as a rock singer." But at a Top 40 rock station the program director claimed, "She has more of a country sound and we're trying to stay away from that." It seemed as if lang was facing a formidable uphill climb.

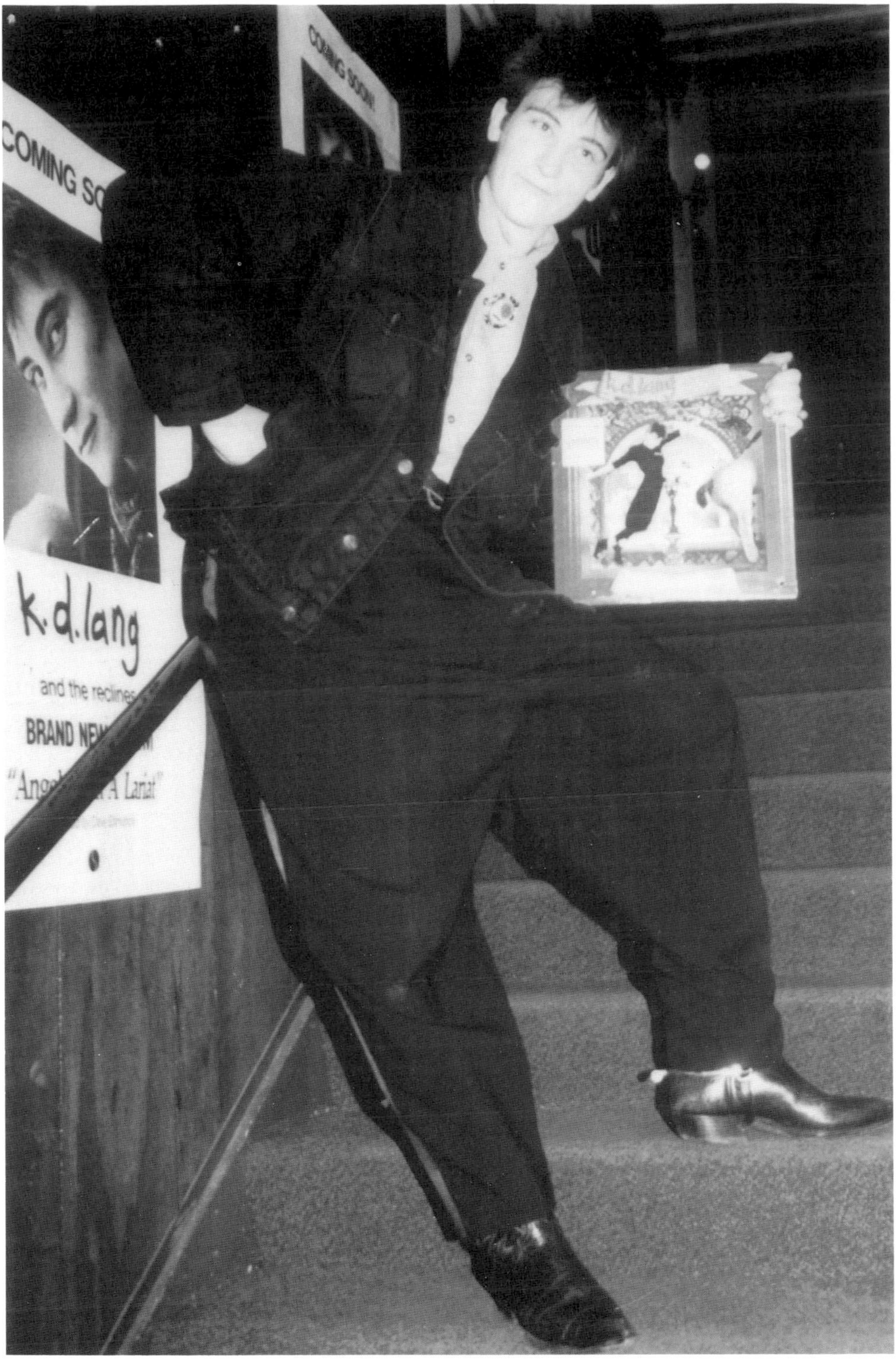
COMING SOON!
k.d.lang
and the reclines

CHAPTER FIVE

PAY DIRT

By the spring of 1985, lang had a debut album with respectable sales and a video of one of the tracks, "Hanky Panky," that was achieving limited national exposure. The "Hanky Panky" video communicated something of lang's audience appeal, showing her at her honky-tonk best, rousing her public off its feet and onto the dance floor. To promote the album and fan their grassroots celebrity flames, k d. lang and the reclines set off on a 16-stop cross-country tour of Canada.

It was at the tour's kickoff at the Western Development Museum in Saskatoon that her future biographer William Robertson, a local concert and record reviewer, caught lang's act. He described the crowd that April night as a curious mix of "boppers, . . . the country crowd in hats and shiny boots, the bikers, ten-speeders, musicians, the local theatre crowd, artists, the whole-grain people, folks in tweed jackets,

lang proudly displays her first major-label album, *Angel with a Lariat*. Disappointingly, producer Dave Edmunds failed to capture her dynamic performing style on tape, and her hard-to-categorize sound confused record marketing executives and radio programmers.

and the gangs that scoured the city, rooting out alternative music." And the diverse audience, Robertson noted, was captivated by what it saw. "She kicked down the doors of people's inhibitions," he recorded, "by looking weirder and wilder than any of them had imagined. She kicked down the doors of their hearts with her soaring, swooping alto, the kind of voice that made even the most puzzled or offended members of the audience forgive and forget as they danced out of themselves and into the palms of lang's hands."

With press clips and video in hand, Richard Flohil, determined to broaden lang's exposure beyond the Canadian club scene and to sniff out a record contract, used his media contacts to get through to Alan Pepper, owner of the famous Bottom Line, a nightclub in New York City renowned for making careers. Pepper agreed to book lang in May on a bill called "Local Heroes," dedicated to largely unknown bands with strong cult followings.

Interrupting their Canadian tour for the New York show, lang and the band electrified the crowd at the Bottom Line on May 2, 1985. Through his contacts, Flohil had also gotten lang a three-quarter-page photo and blurb in *Rolling Stone* magazine, the voice of rock 'n' roll, which had called lang's U.S. debut nothing short of "kinetic." The *Village Voice* also sat up and took notice of what reviewer Leslie Berman called lang's "erratically released energy." Unfortunately, Berman found that all the "writhing," "wiggles," and "soulful sad gazes" made it hard not to watch lang rather than listen to her.

The Bottom Line proved another turning point for lang, though she didn't realize its impact immediately. Her crowd-pleasing performance got her an invitation to return to the club the following month, and record executives who had caught her show were taking notice of her appeal. "She has that sort of special charm that captures you involuntarily," said one record producer. "I was captivated the whole time." Promotional packets containing *A Truly Western Experience* were sent out as feelers to executives, and lang's handlers began getting calls. High on the list of potential record companies was CBS, but a preliminary meeting there disappointed lang, who didn't like their offer or their style. So the longed-for record contract was still not in sight.

lang and the band resumed their Canadian bookings, and "within two weeks," one reporter noted, "Lang had played for more than 25,000 people" at various venues in Toronto. Returning to New York as promised just a few weeks later, the reclines opened at the Bottom Line for NRBQ (New Rhythm and Blues Quartet) and once again brought down the house. That night, however, there was a man in the audience who would finally give lang's career the boost it needed.

Seymour Stein, the head of Sire Records (a division of Warner Brothers), had recruited such distinctive performers as Madonna, Talking Heads, and the Ramones for his label, but he had never signed a country artist. Still, lang's quirky style had appealed to him when he first heard *A Truly Western Experience,* and that night at the Bottom Line he went backstage to congratulate her. lang later recalled that he asked if she knew "Ballad of a Teenage Queen" by Johnny Cash and "She's No Angel" by Kitty Wells.

lang was stunned. She was familiar with Stein's eclectic label, and she could not believe that the man who had signed Madonna knew "all about country music and who played on which records. I just looked at him and it was love at first sight!" Reportedly, what Stein told lang was, "You are what country music would have been if Nashville hadn't screwed it up."

What Stein meant was that the so-called Nashville Sound had become too "wholesome" and commercial. While a performer like lang was a natural descendant of brassy stars like Patsy Cline, Nashville had smoothed over its image in the seventies and produced a sound that was unoriginal and watered down. "What had once been the white equivalent of blues," according to a reporter in *Maclean's,* "was transformed, acquiring so thick a gloss . . . that songs of heartache became music to snicker to." Stein found lang's style refreshing and unique: "What she was doing with country music should have been done thirty years earlier."

The contract with Sire Records/Warner Brothers that resulted was a three-album deal. Signed on a boat in Vancouver Sound the night before lang and her band left to play Expo '85 in Japan, the document promised the kind of time and promotion that lang needed to become

k. d. lang

As she gained a wider audience, lang made some adjustments in her image, discarding her lensless glasses and wearing less thrift-shop clothing; however, she continued to charm audiences with her exuberance, often holding dance contests during a concert.

a star. Even today, lang professes that she was extraordinarily lucky in her choice of a record company, because "Warner Brothers is a very artist-oriented label. . . . It's been a pretty comfortable relationship."

It was in Japan that lang met Ben Mink, a violinist who was playing with Cano, another band on the Expo tour. Within a short time, Mink became lang's songwriting partner, arranger, and close friend. He was, perhaps, the soul mate she had lost when Drifter passed out of her life.

Their family backgrounds were sharply different. Mink had grown up in Toronto, the son of Holocaust survivors and the grandson of a trained Hasidic cantor. But lang and Mink shared a passion for music, a perfectionist streak, and a whimsical sense of humor that lang first recognized when she saw his violin. Inside its body, Mink had glued a tableau of miniature toy figures and plastic farm animals, reminiscent of the plastic cowboys and Indians lang liked to sew onto the skirts of her costumes. "She saw that," he reports, "and said, 'Do you have any songs?'"

Though the press had generally been enchanted by her performing style and her voice, lang was well aware that her songwriting had been pinpointed as a weakness. Her compositions "are of uneven quality," wrote reviewer Liam Lacey, who had gushed over her singing talent, and "[lang] has not yet proven her songwriting ability." Ben Mink was recruited for the reclines to help lang strengthen her songwriting and nurture her creativity. "Ben pointed out something that hit home in a significant way," lang says. "He said that Patsy and Owen Bradley didn't try to re-create. They tried to create. They were doing something new."

Mink reports that he was at first astounded by lang's self-assurance, which had been boosted by her new record deal. "I'm going to be one of the world's biggest stars," he remembers her saying. And, in fact, the months after she returned from Japan found lang soaring headlong toward stardom, even before she started recording for Sire.

Though it was something she had dreamed of and longed for, lang found celebrity hard to adjust to in those early years. Always basically a loner, she was both unused to and fueled by all the public attention. lang tells the story of a traumatic moment when she first started "to experience 'celebritism.' It wasn't easy to take. So I went into the bathroom and cut my hair." In fact, she cut most of it off, exposing her scalp in a bizarre kind of self-mutilation. lang was scheduled to appear on TV a few days later, and having to perform with such a severe and jagged haircut, she says, "humbled me very quickly."

While she waited to record the first album of the new contract, lang had a lot to keep her busy. In November 1985, she had the opportunity to perform in concert with the Edmonton Symphony Orchestra—a seemingly unlikely combination but one that was broadcast coast to coast. That same month lang received a Juno Award, given annually for excellence in the Canadian music industry, for Most Promising Female Vocalist. As lang puts it, "The Canadians decided to anoint me into the Canadian music industry." Accepting her award in Toronto, she bounded onto the stage in outrageous k.d. lang style in a long white wedding dress and veil. With "Hanky Panky" playing in the background, she lifted her dress to dance and stomp around the stage to the hoots and hollers of the audience. Then she kissed the award, caught her breath, and, holding her heart, made a reverent vow (like a bride): "I promise that I'll continue to sing for only the right reasons." With that, she gave what had become her signature "thank you" in both live and taped performances—a bird-dive curtsy on one leg. The wedding dress made such a visual impact and became such a popular image of her in the press that lang subsequently donated the costume to the Canadian Music Hall of Fame in Evanston, Alberta.

Seymour Stein's people at Sire meanwhile had been searching for an appropriate producer for lang's first album. High on their list was Dave Edmunds, a British rock guitarist who had also worked with country stars like Johnny Cash and Carl Perkins. Reluctant at first, Edmunds was finally persuaded to sign on to the project, but only if recording could take place in London. So, in the spring of 1986, k.d. lang and the reclines flew to England to record *Angel with a Lariat.*

The album, which they finished recording in June, was a mix of rockabilly, swing, and polka, and it sadly didn't meet lang's expectations or hopes for her first "real" album. Edmunds had never seen her perform live and was not able to translate her unusual style to vinyl. Everyone involved had a different take on why the experience went sour. "He didn't understand what I was doing," lang says outright of Edmunds, "and I was just so hyper and enthusiastic and overly emotional. I fought everything he said, whether it was right or wrong. I just wanted to get my record out and to be a big star right away." Edmunds also realized that it had not been a good match. "That one," he said of *Angel,* "wasn't really up my street. There were things I didn't understand, like the polkas and the weird stuff she does." Caustically, Ben Mink complained that the English studio and technicians "were far below our standards."

Angel has definite weaknesses and is slower to take to than lang's later recordings. On some of the tracks, like the title cut and "Pay Dirt," lang's pure and distinctive voice is virtually swallowed up by the band. Most memorable among the songs are the rousing "Turn Me 'Round," a new tune by Mink; "Three Cigarettes in an Ashtray," a tear-jerking Patsy Cline torch song that had become a staple of lang's

lang would be onstage "ranting and raving," noted one observer, "and then you'd go backstage to say hi . . . and the person you'd talk to would be real quiet." Sudden celebrity, as well as the blurred boundary between "Kathy" and "k.d.," exerted new pressures on lang.

live performances; and a rocking cover of Lynn Anderson's 1970 hit "Rose Garden," which became the first single Sire released for airplay. The yearning "Diet of Strange Places" foreshadows lang's later "Constant Craving" with its lyrics about "starving," "hunger," and "a craving that wears me thin."

The album cover successfully illustrated the quirkiness that fans had come to expect of her, and lang herself played a major role in its art direction. On the front, lang—wearing the simple black dress from her "Sun Country" performance—flies past an archway decorated with cutout angels and guitars. On one side of the album sleeve, lang appears in a derby and string tie while in the field of haystacks behind her, the reclines dance with white cardboard cowgirls. It is k.d. lang at her offbeat best.

Following the recording of *Angel* but prior to its release, lang made her first appearances on U.S. television. In September 1986, she debuted on "Late Night with David Letterman," where she would be a guest six times in as many years. Subsequently, the producers of the country show "Hee Haw" invited her to appear for a two-song set, then were so impressed with her that they let her perform four numbers.

To promote *Angel,* which was released the following March, lang and the band embarked on a six-month tour of Canada and the United States as the opening act for country artist Dwight Yoakam. Opinion about lang's new record was mixed, with the U.S. reviewers tending to prefer her live performances to the album. Indeed, *Variety* proclaimed her a "virtuoso," who "belted, growled, keened and delivered the blues."

But many didn't know what to make of her eccentricities. The question in a lot of people's minds was, how earnest was k.d. lang about music in general and country music in particular? Was she more of a performance artist than a serious vocalist? The question would trail lang for years. Her work often did seem to jump over the line into parody. When lang revealed the "comic undertones" of a classic like "Three Cigarettes in an Ashtray"— literally adding and removing cigarettes from an ashtray as she sang- -some country music aficionados saw it as dangerously close to blasphemy.

Besides her country humor, on tour lang liked to do a sixties pop song, "Johnny Get Angry," which had always been a hit for her in clubs. It was hard to believe, hearing lang's tongue-in-cheek performance of the song in the 1980s, that any woman had ever seriously sung the lyrics, "Johnny get angry/Johnny get mad . . . I want a brave man/I want a cave man." lang's updated interpretation, in which she threw her body around the stage, feigning abuse, was decidedly feminist and made a lot of people uncomfortable.

lang's controversial style embraced a yin-yang type of philosophy. "I like to incorporate humor and emotion into a song at the same time," she explained. "For me, life is about opposites."

Angel peaked at only number 56 on *Billboard*'s Top Country Albums chart, hurt by its failure to draw the radio airplay so critical to a record's success. It was not a bad showing, but hardly enough to make lang a full-fledged star. As reporter Michael Corcoran put it, "The rock stations wouldn't play her because she was too country, and the country stations wouldn't touch her because she was, um, strange. . . . The good-ol'-boy network is tough to crack, especially for a woman in a buzz haircut and sawed-off cowboy boots who does sacrilegious takes on Lynn Anderson."

Since humor had always been a part of the country music tradition (and a show like "Hee Haw" was evidence of it), it seemed that something deeper was troubling the country establishment about lang— and Corcoran's use of "um, strange" would be a sign of things to come. Her inability to get much-needed airplay would haunt lang's country career and eventually embitter her toward Nashville.

But in 1987, on the brink of realizing her dream, k.d. lang was hopeful that, if the badly executed and ill-fated *Angel with a Lariat* could not do it, the next album would catapult her into stardom.

CHAPTER SIX

HONKY TONK
ANGEL

When I first got to Nashville, I was given a pink handbook on how to be a country-and-western star. Section 1A, the first rule of country-and-western stardom, is, "The higher the hair, the closer to God." I tried but it just wasn't me.

Nashville, Tennessee, is to country music what Hollywood is to movies or New York is to publishing. In 1925, Nashville's radio station WSM (one of only two in the South with over 1,000 watts of power) began airing a weekly country barn dance in a small studio in downtown Nashville. "For the past hour," host George D. Hay announced, "we have been listening to music taken largely from grand opera, but from now on we will present the Grand Ole Opry." People from all over the South thronged the studio wanting to hear the performances live, and the Grand Ole Opry moved to larger and larger auditoriums in Nashville to accommodate the crowds. Even during the Great Depression, when few people could really afford the 25 cent

lang suavely croons on public television's "Center Stage." In 1987 *Billboard* reviewer Gerry Wood quipped, "If Patsy Cline and Elvis Presley had conceived a daughter, her name would probably be k.d. lang."

admission, fans averaged 3,000 a week. The Grand Ole Opry quickly became the most popular and revered of country music venues.

After World War II, Nashville's hold on the country music arena was further consolidated when Decca Records producer Owen Bradley and his brother built the first large recording studio there in 1952, on what would become known as Music Row. It was one of the most technically advanced studios in the region. Soon other studios followed, and with them all the people needed to turn Nashville into Music City—music publishers, musicians, singers, booking agents, songwriters.

But Nashville is also home to the Southern Baptist Convention and Thomas Nelson, the world's largest publisher of Bibles, and southern white, churchgoing conservatism has had a powerful impact on the country music business, especially since the social and political upheavals of the 1960s. A passionate and sometimes violent intolerance of difference marks the politics of southern whites and has manifested itself in racism, anticommunism, antifeminism, and homophobia. The Religious Right stresses patriotism, prayer, and conformity to "traditional family values," and the music that has come out of Nashville in the last 30 years largely reflects this reactionary spirit—right is right, wrong is wrong, and men and women have prescribed roles to play. Given Nashville's history, it was no wonder the country music establishment reeled when it came face to face with a new style of country artist like k.d. lang.

k.d. lang first saw Nashville when she filmed a segment of "Hee Haw" there in late 1986, before *Angel with a Lariat* was released. Exhilarated to be in Patsy's town, lang soaked up the atmosphere at Cline's favorite haunts, like Ernest Tubb's Record Shop, the Ryman Auditorium (where the Grand Ole Opry broadcast from 1943 to 1974), and Tootsie's Orchid Lounge. At Tootsie's, where the tradition is for visitors to sign their names on the walls amid the photographs of Nashville's stars, lang reportedly found Patsy's picture and put her signature on the wall right next to it. Being there was the closest she had ever been to Cline.

In April of 1987, to promote *Angel,* lang made a second trip to Nashville, this time for a live performance at the Exit/In, a famous Nashville club. Sire invited the elite of the Nashville music scene, and the crowd rewarded lang with two standing ovations. Among those who cheered lang that evening were Wynonna Judd, Bonnie Raitt, Juice Newton, and many from the "Hee Haw" cast, including Minnie Pearl, one of the regulars.

Minnie Pearl was a flamboyant comedian, a 75-year-old Nashville veteran who had made her mark with her self-mocking portrayal of a country bumpkin in a straw hat with a price tag dangling from the brim.

Ernest Tubb and the Texas Troubadors broadcast a performance from the Grand Ole Opry's Ryman Auditorium in the 1940s. Despite Nashville's conservatism, lang's 1987 debut at the Grand Ole Opry was a smash.

k. d. lang

A shriek of "How-DEE!" was her trademark stage entrance. Pearl's brand of comedy was a direct ancestor to lang's tongue-in-cheek musical renditions, and Sire decided to stage a meeting for the two at the Country Music Hall of Fame as a promotional piece. Taped by a crew from the television show "Entertainment Tonight," Pearl gave lang a private tour of the museum, which included a stop at the Patsy Cline exhibit.

The admiration between lang and Pearl was mutual, and Pearl proved one of lang's fiercest champions in Nashville. It was not just lang's "pure, beautiful" voice that impressed Pearl; it was also that "there is nothing phony about her. . . . I think k.d. represents the freedom we wish we all had."

Pearl was so taken with lang that she helped her get a spot on the Grand Ole Opry in October 1987. Sharing a matinee bill with perennial host Roy Acuff, Pearl, and George Hamilton IV, lang brought the 4,400-seat house down with just one song and was then summoned back by the thundering crowd for an encore. Her brief performance, according to Judy Bryte, an agent who books talent at the Opry, "slaughtered them." Backstage, Acuff told lang, "You look like a boy, dress like a girl, and sing like a bird."

The combination of her success at the Grand Ole Opry and an interview on the Nashville talk show "Crook and Chase" helped make lang a more familiar name in the country music mecca. Appearing on "Crook and Chase" several times over the next couple of years, lang delighted the studio audiences with her unconventional entrances—one time, walking onstage backward; the next, sticking her head through the curtain, asking "Hey, where are the stairs?" Co-host Lorraine Crook told lang, "We love having you on the show, k.d., because we never know what you're going to do." When the hosts asked about her unorthodox look, lang replied simply, "I think country music has a tradition of promoting honesty, and honest, down-to-earth people, and although I might not be from this particular earth, I'm just being honest."

Another of lang's allies at this time was the celebrated Roy Orbison, who, late in 1987, invited her to record a duet of his classic "Crying"

Like lang, singer-songwriter Roy Orbison, pictured with his wife, Barbara, successfully straddled the country and pop music worlds. lang found the experience of singing with Orbison richly rewarding.

tor the sound track of the film *Hiding Out*. Orbison was a living legend both in country music and in rock 'n' roll, renowned for such songs as "Pretty Woman" and "Only the Lonely." To be invited to sing with him was an enormous honor.

lang now calls the chance to work with Orbison a "blessing" and the man himself her "personal prophet," but at first she was reluctant to make the record. "I said it should be either Roy singing or me singing. . . . [Then] I started to wake up and go, 'It's Roy Orbison that you'll be singing with, you goon.'"

lang describes Orbison as "very silent but very strong." While recording the duet of "Crying," they shared a microphone and were standing so close that their cheeks brushed. "His cheeks were just so, so soft, and yet his body was providing this enormous sound."

The duet climbed the country charts and gave lang even greater exposure. Later, the two filmed a video of their collaboration. In the spring of 1988, Orbison invited lang to perform the song with him again on his HBO special, "A Black and White Night," which also featured Elvis Costello, Jackson Browne, Bonnie Raitt, and Bruce Springsteen. "Everything I did with Roy brought baskets of horseshoes," lang later commented. When Orbison died unexpectedly in December 1988, lang inherited "Crying" as her own, and she has performed it countless times to standing ovations. One concert reviewer speculated that "'Crying' could become her 'Over the Rainbow.'"

In all, 1987 proved a banner year for k.d. lang. Though she was still not a household name in the United States, Canada recognized her talent with a string of awards. lang's second Juno Award, this time for Best Country Female Vocalist of 1987, shut out her former idol, Anne Murray, for the first time in eight years. The Canadian Country Music Association proclaimed lang Entertainer of the Year and also presented her with a Vista Rising Star Award. Just before her 26th birthday in November, *Angel with a Lariat* went gold in Canada, selling a half million copies.

And one performance that year would prove especially important for lang's future. Making her debut on the "Tonight Show with Johnny Carson" on May 27, 1987, lang had her usual strong audience appeal, singing a heartfelt version of Patsy Cline's "Three Cigarettes in an Ashtray." She charmed not only the audience but also Johnny Carson himself, who extended her an open invitation to appear on the "Tonight Show" whenever she wanted.

What was most significant about that television performance was that Owen Bradley, one of the creators of the Nashville Sound and the producer of all of Patsy Cline's hits, had tuned into Carson that night. Bradley, 72 and in retirement since 1980, was recovering in a Nash- ville hospital from a heart attack when k.d. lang's performance made him sit up and take notice. Though Bradley had already received a publicity copy of *Angel with a Lariat,* it was not until he heard lang on the "Tonight Show" that he realized her potential, which had not fully come across to him on *Angel*. lang's talent was great enough to coax the legendary producer out of convalescence and back into the recording studio. Bradley later wrote in the liner notes of their collaboration, *Shadowland,* "To me she was medicine . . . invigorating therapy after an illness of mine. After working with k.d. for a while, I didn't need to take my pills."

Owen Bradley was another living legend who showered "baskets of horseshoes" on k.d. lang. If anyone could make a career in Nashville, it was the man who had built the first Nashville recording studio and produced not only the great Patsy Cline but also Loretta Lynn, Kitty Wells, Ernest Tubb, Red Foley, and Brenda Lee. With Chet Atkins, Don Law, and Anita Kerr, Bradley had created the "Nashville Sound" in the 1950s, which smoothed over the rough hillbilly edges of country music and made it more competitive with pop. The Nashville Sound was widely heralded as the savior of country music. So when Bradley agreed to produce lang's next album, "it was magical," lang says.

The recording of *Shadowland: The Owen Bradley Sessions* took place at Bradley's Barn, Bradley's recording studio on his farm in Mt. Juliet, Tennessee. lang was to record this time without the reclines, because Bradley, a former big band leader, preferred working with his own network of musicians and backup vocalists to create the rich, orchestral arrangements that had made him famous as one of the architects of the Nashville Sound.

"I think the reclines were put off at first," lang later said, "but I think they realize now it was an opportunity I had to fulfill." By then, the band included only one original member, guitarist Gordie Matthews.

The album included a host of country standards chosen by Bradley and lang, mixed in with jazz and pop. lang later told *Canadian Musician* that one reason she was eager to work with Bradley was his ability to select songs. "He's really into straight ahead lyrics . . . and subject matter everyone can understand. It's almost a totally different school from where I come from. He's opened me up."

In the studio, Bradley would play songs for lang on the piano until they found ones that she wanted to record, like "I Wish I Didn't

k. d. lang

Beloved country performer Loretta Lynn deals openly with women's issues in such songs as "Fist City" and "The Pill." lang kept Lynn's picture nearby for inspiration while recording *Shadowland.*

Love You So," "Don't Let the Stars Get In Your Eyes," and "Lock, Stock, and Teardrops." On her own, lang chose "Western Stars," by a young California songwriter, and "Black Coffee," a Peggy Lee tune that lang loved.

The title cut, "Shadowland," was one of Bradley's old big band numbers. "Here's a great song, k.d.," Bradley said, playing it for her, "but I don't think it's singable." "That put a burr under my saddle," lang relates, and she practiced the complex tune until she had mastered it. "The title of the song became the title of the album," lang later said, "because it incorporates the way I feel about being in the shadow of Patsy Cline and in the shadow of great vocalists."

lang and Bradley developed an easy approach to working with the songs they chose for the album. "Once we selected the material we'd practice," lang remembers. "Just him on piano and me singing. We'd only practice a song two or three times in a day, and the rest of the day, which would be about five hours, we would spend listening to great jazz vocalists like Carmen McRae, Ella, and Peggy Lee." During these listening sessions, Bradley also introduced lang to hillbilly singers and musicians he admired. "What we really did was start a communication system on what we liked and what we thought was weak about vocal styles."

The closing track of the album was "Honky Tonk Angels' Medley," a composite of three country standards sung in harmony with Nashville stars Loretta Lynn, Kitty Wells, and Brenda Lee. It was Bradley's idea to unite the four artists, and it marked the first time that Lynn, Wells, and Lee had ever performed together. The symbolic stamp of approval of three of country's greatest singers was designed to represent lang's admittance into the Nashville community. The video made of the historic recording session shows the four enjoying each other's company as they blend their talents and voices. The older women were impressed with lang's voice and style.

"I hadn't seen a woman work like that in a long time!" Brenda Lee said of the experience. "She's a great singer but she's very uninhibited, not afraid to try new things. . . . Not much intimidates her."

"She's got the talent," Kitty Wells added. "She doesn't need to be intimidated by anybody!"

"Greatness doesn't intimidate," lang explained. "Working with great people, you feel honored, humbled, and blessed."

Later, lang detailed what it was like to work with the three celebrated country singers. "Brenda is a very technical singer, Kitty is so serene and maternal, and Loretta is exactly what you thought she'd be like. She came into the studio with a pound of bologna and a loaf of white bread, and everyone had bologna sandwiches. I'm a vegetarian, but I almost ate one. I thought it was blessed food."

In fact, the whole experience of creating *Shadowland* bordered on being a religious one for lang, in large part because it was the culmination of her dream "to get close to Patsy Cline and to the influences I had felt in that direction." Working with Bradley was "as close as I would get to Patsy on this earth. It's a difficult thing to talk about—it's rather like explaining how you feel about God." It was such an emotional experience for lang that, she says, "It took me a while to adjust after I made that record."

After *Shadowland*, the ghost of Patsy Cline left lang. "When I finished that album," she told reporter Liam Lacey, "the whole Patsy thing somehow came to an end. . . . I think, in a way, that *Shadowland* was the whole reason for the Patsy obsession, and now I can just go back to being k.d. lang."

lang shares the stage with country legends Brenda Lee, Loretta Lynn, and Kitty Wells as they rehearse their memorable collaboration, "Honky Tonk Angels' Medley," for the 1988 Country Music Association Awards show.

Shadowland was released in May 1988 and shot into the country music charts. As hoped, it also crossed over into the pop charts, proving that lang had the wider appeal that a select group of country stars had enjoyed. Pop critics especially loved the album, and *Rolling Stone* observed that lang "sets off explosions on almost every song." Another reviewer agreed that lang "doesn't sing this material so much as inhabit it. . . . She delivers with an explosion of emotion."

In general, the album was a more conservative vehicle for lang than either *A Truly Western Experience* or *Angel with a Lariat*. Gone were the homemade album covers, the bustling polkas, the campy lyrics. The only song on the album with any comic relief was "Waltz Me Once Again Around the Dance Floor," and even that was a far cry from lang's earlier style of comedy. lang's image, too, was toned down from outrageous country satire to a more "serious" Nashville look. She was playing as close to Nashville's rules as she could without sacrificing her integrity.

It was a stunning album, and with the combined forces of Owen Bradley, Loretta Lynn, Kitty Wells, and Brenda Lee behind her, lang and her record company expected the country music establishment to throw aside their past reservations about lang's commitment and her appearance. But the shocking reality was that Nashville would not embrace lang even after the rave reviews and the blessings of the heavy hitters. Country radio stations virtually ignored the album. "It's a very big disappointment that it didn't get played more," Bradley complained. "I can't explain it." Only two cuts on *Shadowland* received any airplay, the traditionally country "I'm Down to My Last Cigarette" and the torchy "Lock, Stock, and Teardrops."

Airplay is crucial to an album's sales, and country radio playlists wield enormous power. Country music stations in the United States number more than 2,500 and are more prevalent than any other kind of station. "It used to be that each station had its own identity," Bradley remembered. In the early 1950s, Loretta Lynn and her husband drove from country station to country station with copies of her first single in hand, charming disc jockeys into playing it. "Now there's 10,000 stations in America," Bradley says, "and you drive down the road and they're all playing the same thing. It gets so homogenized it's in-distinguishable."

Bradley later outlined why he thought lang was running into a brick wall in the country music establishment. "I was in Atlanta," he told *Saturday Night* magazine, "and some of the people there, they love the songs, but they don't like the image. That comes up quite a bit. . . . You can fight the flow—sometimes it attracts more attention to fight the flow—but you pay a price for that. k.d. fights it. I think she's winning slowly but surely. She's just outsinging them . . . and that's the hardest way to go."

Without airplay, singers and musicians have to rely on concert tours, TV appearances, and print interviews to promote their albums. With its complicated orchestral arrangements, *Shadowland* was a difficult album to translate to stage performances, and lang toured only a few major cities, opening for Lyle Lovett. For promotion, she relied instead on exposure from repeated appearances on the "Tonight Show" and from an HBO special called "Country Music: A New Tradition." The show featured artists like lang, Roseanne Cash, and the Judds working alongside an older generation of singers, including Waylon Jennings, Carl Perkins, and Merle Haggard. lang performed "Lock, Stock, and Teardrops" with the Jordanaires, who had also sung backup for Patsy Cline, Elvis Presley, and a host of Nashville greats, and joined Roseanne Cash for a duet of Loretta Lynn's "You Ain't Woman Enough To Take My Man."

Despite the cold shoulder of country radio stations, *Shadowland* sold very well, going platinum in Canada (100,000 units) and gold internationally. "I think I've been successful," lang said, though her frustration with the country music world would soon turn into hostility. "I play to sold-out audiences and I play my music in uncompromising terms." But in a late-1988 interview in *Canadian Musician* magazine, lang bitterly voiced her resentment, noting that the U.S. country music scene was filled with "rednecks."

In a big surprise for both lang and Sire Records, the singer received three Grammy Award nominations for 1988: Best Female Country Vocalist for "I'm Down to My Last Cigarette," and Best Country Music

Collaboration for both "Crying" and "Honky Tonk Angels' Medley." If lang was shocked by the nominations, she was completely stunned when she actually won the award for "Crying." Though her acceptance was not part of the televised Grammys, lang accepted the award with Orbison's widow. "Just singing with Roy was rewarding enough," lang said with great emotion.

The Grammy Awards, however, are bestowed by the recording industry in Los Angeles. *Shadowland,* a country masterpiece, was completely overlooked by the Nashville-sponsored Country Music Awards, though lang was invited to perform at the awards ceremony. It was beginning to look doubtful that lang could ever really crack the hard shell that surrounded Nashville.

CHAPTER SEVEN

THE TWANG'S
THE THANG

While still having difficulty getting airplay in the States, k.d. lang had no trouble accumulating kudos in her native Canada. Early in 1988 the Canadian women's magazine *Chatelaine* proclaimed her their Woman of the Year. Similar to *Vogue* in the United States, *Chatelaine* was not prone to honoring women like lang, who were not traditionally glamorous and made it a strict policy not to wear makeup. "It was quite a big step for them to put someone like me on the cover," said lang, "because I'm not a stereotypical woman. . . . I think it's great because they allowed me to be myself."

At the last minute, though, an editor or art director at the magazine must have gotten cold feet about putting the barefaced lang on the cover. When the issue hit the newsstands, lang's lips had been airbrushed with red lipstick. "I guess that was their last laugh," lang later mused. Perhaps a desire to get her own "last

lang acknowledges the cheers of a loyal Canadian audience. One of Canada's most popular performers, she was asked to sing at the closing ceremonies of the 1988 Winter Olympics in Calgary.

81

laugh" led lang to satirize the honor on her *Ingenue* album, in the song "Miss Chatelaine." "I can't explain," lang crooned, "why I've become Miss Chatelaine."

In February 1988, lang was asked to perform at the closing ceremonies of the Winter Olympics in Calgary, Alberta. She later called it one of the highlights of her career. With 2 billion people watching worldwide, lang felt both jittery and high on adrenaline. In the enormous stadium, lang, in a bright red cowgirl dress, was introduced to the 60,000 audience members as "the Alberta Rose, the pride of the west." Prancing and twirling onto the stage while skaters and dancers in fringed western costumes circled her, lang delivered a boisterous rendition of "Turn Me 'Round" from *Angel with a Lariat.* Athletes spontaneously swarmed from the stands and square-danced their way right onto the field and the stage. At the end of the dynamic performance, lang flashed the two-fingered peace sign from the sixties and wished the crowd "peace on earth."

Canada continued to honor "the Alberta Rose" later that year with triple awards at the Canadian Country Music Awards. lang won Entertainer of the Year, Best Female Vocalist, and Album of the Year for *Shadowland*. In her acceptance, she described *Shadowland* as a gift and thanked the reclines for the time off to record with Owen Bradley. That year, lang also picked up a CASBY (Canadian Artists Selected by You), comparable to the American Music Awards in the United States. Unlike other Canadians who head south when celebrity hits, lang remained a Canadian citizen, moving her residence from Alberta to Vancouver, British Columbia, in 1988.

There was hardly a chance to breathe before k.d. lang was back in the recording studio with the reclines, taping her fourth album, *Absolute Torch and Twang*. lang coined the phrase "torch and twang" to describe the hybrid style of her music. The press had classified her as everything from "cowpunk" to "rockabilly" to "new traditionalist." Where, exactly, did she fit in the progression of country music? "Cowpunk" suggested the humor of lang's music and the frenetic energy she displayed onstage, and "rockabilly" referred to the rock music with a hillbilly twist that Elvis and others had popularized.

The style of the "new traditionalists"—performers such as Roseanne Cash and the Judds—was stripped of the artificial urban gloss Nashville had used to obscure the roots of country music and make it more competitive with pop music.

But lang was dissatisfied with all the labels that compartmentalized country music performers. lang wanted to "open things up" and allow herself the flexibility to create a style of music that did not fit any of the categories. "Torch songs are what attract me," she explained, "and the twang comes from the instruments I use. It's a term flexible enough to take me anywhere I want to go."

In a Sire Records promotional still, lang shows off her unique brand of country chic. A *Nashville Banner* reviewer enthused that lang had given "country music a tornado of a twirl that could send a few rhinestones flying into the 21st century."

k. d. lang

lang's goal was to make a unique contribution to country music. Not a pure country artist, lang had been influenced as much by jazz singers like Dinah Washington and Peggy Lee as by Patsy Cline. "I would love to marry ballad jazz and country," lang explained. "People have incorporated jazz into country before, but I don't think anyone's dedicated their life to it."

A brilliant mix of styles and tempos, *Absolute Torch and Twang* is perhaps lang's finest album. This time, lang herself co-produced the album with Ben Mink and Greg Penny, a young producer whose mother, Sue Thompson, had recorded in Nashville in the 1950s and 1960s. lang chose a studio in Vancouver, and she wrote 8 of the 12 songs with Mink and one by herself. Unlike the ill-fated *Angel with a Lariat,* it was a project very much under her control.

The songs have a distinctly autobiographical feel, from the moment lang sings the opening track, "Luck in My Eyes": "Gonna walk away

lang's nonconformist appearance continued to disturb the country music establishment despite the critical and commercial success of *Absolute Torch and Twang.* Ready to explore other musical avenues, she reluctantly concluded, "I'm not prepared to make the kind of compromises that would be necessary for me to be accepted by those people. . . . They make their own assessments whether you're honest or not."

from trouble with my head held high/Then look closely you'll see luck in my eyes."

With a strong feminist slant, "Wallflower Waltz" and "Big Boned Gal" both portray women rarely seen in country or pop music. "Usually, a country song about a wallflower expresses sympathy. This was more of a celebration," lang explained. "There's a little bit of a wallflower in everyone." "Big Boned Gal," which celebrates a big, proud woman "with a bounce in her step and a wiggle in her walk," quickly became a rebel anthem for lesbians. Big, sassy women had never been saluted with such relish before.

Also notable on the album is the poignant "Nowhere To Stand," which made lang one of only a handful of songwriters ever to tackle the subject of child abuse. Though she would later claim that she did not want to use her music as a vehicle for politics, the song was a strong statement that lang must have known would further alienate country music stations.

In *Rolling Stone* magazine, Holly Gleason characterized the feeling of the new album. "This album isn't going to win her any points with the Nashville Network or country-radio programmers," Gleason wrote, "but it shows what country music, when intelligently done, can be: high-plains music for the thinking man and woman."

"High-plains music" was an accurate assessment. The cover of the album featured a photograph of lang in an expansive Alberta wheat field, wearing blue jeans and a leather jacket, holding a white cowboy hat, and turning up her determined chin proudly toward miles of blue sky. Though not in itself a tribute to Alberta, the album definitely drew its inspiration from lang's upbringing in the western province. "This is where I'm from," lang explained, "and this is where most of the imagery in my music and performance comes from. And most of my humor is Canadian." *Absolute Torch and Twang,* lang told *Canadian Living* magazine, was, in fact, "the first time I have ever truly revealed that many aspects of me: the writing, the production, being absolutely myself on the cover."

Absolute Torch and Twang, released in spring 1989, was a hit with lang's fans as well as with reviewers. To promote the album, lang and the reclines embarked on an exhausting tour that kicked off in North Carolina and wound its way up the East Coast, through the Midwest, and into Canada. Night after night they played to sold-out houses. At New York's Beacon Theater, lang received a standing ovation for her first song, "Big Big Love," and the audience brought her back for five encores. "Those who witnessed it were baptized," wrote the ecstatic *New York Times* reviewer. "k.d. is God."

But it was not an album the country radio stations embraced. lang had probably already figured out that if *Shadowland,* her most traditional and conservative album to date, had not won the hearts of country music stations, her problems with Nashville ran deep. "It's a weird paradox," lang mused. "I'm accepted artistically in Nashville. I performed on the CMA [Country Music Association] Awards, but I'm not nominated for any. Country is intimidated by me or scared."

The country stations were evasive about the lack of airplay, claiming that they played what the public wanted. "I think the lady has a complex," said one radio station manager. "She's got to face the fact that if she's going to be the Boy George of the country music scene, she's going to get some snippy comments." Equating her with the gender-bending Boy George (who later would also come out as gay) was especially revealing. A lot of country music fans, another program director stated, "like a girl to look like a girl and a guy to look like a guy."

"She is the best singer of the decade," said one country music executive. "If she doesn't become a superstar it will be because of her, not her voice. We did a Brenda Lee special and at the end they sang 'America the Beautiful' and, you know, you'd have to be a communist not to stand up. Well, k.d. didn't stand up. She was the only one." Her nontraditional look, combined with the fact that she was Canadian, not American-born, were enough to affect her country music career.

"I think country radio suspected she was a lesbian, and even if they weren't sure, the image was all wrong," said lang's manager, Larry Wanagas. "They weren't about to put k.d. on a pedestal and use her as a role model for all the young women who want to be country music stars."

Barbara Orbison, Roy Orbison's widow, and k.d. lang accept the Grammy Award for Best Country Vocal Collaboration in 1989. "Crying" has since become one of lang's signature pieces.

"It's hard to second-guess radio," lang commented. "I could grow my hair, wear pretty little dresses and then go around to all the country stations. Gimmicks don't make it with me."

It would be easy to dismiss the radio stations as simply homophobic, but the issue is much more complicated than that. Other country artists have run into problems because Nashville is a town that likes singers to "pay their dues." Many artists, Patsy Cline included, have found that they couldn't make any real inroads into country music until they actually moved to Nashville, the move being the ultimate sign of a "serious" commitment. The 1991 *Songwriter's and Musician's Guide to Nashville* states categorically, "Everyone expects you to move there if you're going to make it." On the surface, this sounds dictatorial, but it is important to remember how many aspiring actors find it necessary to move to Los Angeles and writers to New York in order to "make it" in their careers.

Once an artist is in Nashville, the rule of thumb in the Bible Belt town goes something like this: be Christian, be white, be heterosexual, be family-oriented, be American, be conservative, and for women

(in the immortal words of Tammy Wynette), "stand by your man."
"Country music is very old-school, male-dominated, Christian-oriented. It's probably everything that I'm not," lang observed. And what it boils down to in Nashville, as in other conservative white southern towns, is an antagonism to difference on many levels. "Nashville is an ugly little city," a fed-up k.d. lang declared. In fact, it is a hypocritical town, since the lives of most country music stars do not match (and never have) its ideal—extramarital affairs, divorces, alcoholism, and drug abuse fill the pages of many biographies.

Another rule: Don't poke fun at Nashville unless you have already been accepted. Lyle Lovett, who had recorded a campy version of Wynette's "Stand By Your Man," had also, like lang, had a hard time getting airplay. lang maintains that she understood and appreciated the venerable history of humor in country music, which others in the industry wanted to downplay. "I think that during the attempt to urbanize country music," she hypothesizes, "it [the real nature of country music] got shoved back into the closet and people were offended or afraid that I was trying to nullify its progression, when I was actually trying to add to it."

Some breaches of faith may be forgiven when country artists have become big enough and accepted enough. Garth Brooks, country music's shiniest star, recorded a song in 1993 in direct reaction against the hate-mongering "family values" crusade at the Republican National Convention in 1992, which particularly vilified gay people. Brooks's song, "We Shall Be Free," envisioned a world without discrimination, including that based on sexual orientation. "My thinking is that if I get shot down for this," Brooks stated boldly, "I need to be away from the people who object." It was always clear, though, that Brooks himself, with his wife and baby behind him, was not gay.

The country music establishment has also had a long-standing bias against the women performers in its ranks. "Women performers don't sell tickets" or "women singers don't sell records" were the business prejudices that began developing after World War II, when women in general were being exhorted to abandon careers, get married, and have children. Country music stations contrived an unspoken rule: never play two records by women in a row, because an anonymous "public," they claimed, just didn't want to hear women artists.

Country star Kathy Mattea complains that this anti-woman bias still persists. "There are a lot of radio stations that say, 'I'll play four women's records at a time. I can't add another woman to my playlist until I drop one,'" she told reporter Bob Oermann. While the stations maintain that their playlists are dictated by their listeners, the prejudice against women seems to run deep within the country music business. Between 1967 and the early 1990s, for example, the Country Music Association awarded its highest honor, Entertainer of the Year, only five times to women.

Running counter to this industry sexism is a strong tradition of feminism in country music writing. But independent women like Loretta Lynn, who has written and performed such feminist songs as "The Pill," an ardent endorsement of birth control, would hesitate to tag the label "feminist" on themselves. As writer Don Gillmor has noted, women like Lynn have always demonstrated "a reassuring rather than a threatening strength." For all their gutsiness, for all their "liberated" lyrics, female country stars have not questioned the institution of heterosexuality through their appearance or their music.

Perhaps naively, k.d. lang held onto the idea for a long time that the honesty of country people and country music would win out over the narrow-mindedness she encountered. She was, after all, just a small-town girl herself. What lang stressed was that she had to be true to herself, and that honesty had drawn her to country music in the first place. "I'm aware of how alternative my looks are in comparison with other women," she told reporter Bob Oermann. "I get flak for it. . . . But what is paradoxical about it to me is that country's always been this vehicle for honesty. I've been like this all my life. I dressed like this when I was five."

When *Absolute Torch and Twang* won a Grammy Award for Best Female Country Performance of the year despite the album's lack of airplay, it was a triumph for lang over the dogmatism of Nashville. But she would soon come up against even uglier bigotry, as radio stations found one more reason to repudiate her—for her zealous vegetarianism.

CHAPTER EIGHT

MEAT STINKS

I try not to use my music as a vehicle. . . .
I don't make political statements onstage every night.

k.d. lang has rarely dealt with social or political issues overtly in her music. "Nowhere To Stand," the impassioned plea against child abuse on *Absolute Torch and Twang*, was a notable exception. Instead, the singer has volunteered her name and talents to causes that she strongly believes in. In the fall of 1989, lang bumped back the starting date for recording *Absolute Torch and Twang* so she could perform to a sold-out crowd in Toronto for the Amnesty International Human Rights Now! tour with Sting, Tracy Chapman, and Bruce Springsteen. In later years, she donated performances in benefit concerts for AIDS funding.

lang pets Lulu the cow as she lets viewers know that "Meat Stinks" in a public service announcement for People for the Ethical Treatment of Animals (PETA). The 1990 pro-vegetarian ad ignited a firestorm of controversy in cattle country.

In mid 1990, lang decided to tape a promotional public service announcement (PSA) for the grassroots animal rights organization People for the Ethical Treatment of Animals (PETA). At that time lang had been a strident vegetarian for almost 10 years, since her college days in Red Deer. Growing up in cattle country, working summers as a teenager on local farms, lang had had plenty of time to think about the way animals were treated. "One day I was on a fifteen-mile cattle drive over 250 acres," she remembers. "We were rounding up about fifty head. And I'm throwing comments to the ranchers like, 'Oh, these poor cattle. I wonder if they know what their destinies are.' And these ranchers thought I was a wacky cult member or something. Then it just occurred to me if you planted 250 acres of soybeans, how many people you could feed. It's just too evident, and when I'm there and I see all this, it's very alarming."

At the time she decided to tape the spot for PETA, lang had not yet completely stopped wearing leather, though she had given up almost every leather item in her wardrobe one by one except for her cherished boots. Even her dog was a vegetarian, eating only couscous, soy protein, garlic, and broccoli.

"It's not a fad for me," lang has said of her vegetarianism, "it's a religion." Vegetarianism is the base of lang's spirituality, a pantheistic approach to life that sees connections among all things in nature. "If you spend two hours reading your book, I'll spend two hours reading the way a bug will crawl up a leaf. I really spend more time in nature than anywhere else. I learn from nature."

A few years before the PETA commercial, lang said she preferred the "silent example" of her vegetarianism, trying not to lecture others about eating meat. But by 1990 lang described herself as "militant" about animal rights and was ready to persuade others about her beliefs. Rock star Melissa Etheridge was one of her recruits. "I stayed with her a couple of weeks," Etheridge notes, "and since then I've been unable to touch meat." As a subtle propaganda technique, the newsletter of lang's official fan club, Obvious Gossip, often includes information about lang's animal rights activism and PETA and is splashed with recipes for meat-free dishes such as Iced Beet Soup, Tofu Loaf, Cashew Nut Roast, and Tomato Soup with Basil.

"My number one protectionistic energy goes toward animals maybe even before women," lang startled feminist fans by saying in an interview in *Ms.* magazine. "If people could respect animals, they might respect themselves more. . . ." Given the deep level of her commitment to the issue, it was a logical next step for lang to endorse one of the most tireless animal rights groups in the country.

Founded in 1980, People for the Ethical Treatment of Animals organizes public demonstrations and "zaps" (staged events designed to grab media attention) against the fur and meat trades, and it places undercover spies in laboratories to monitor and report on experiments on animals. The organization has grown rapidly to almost half a million members strong. Some of PETA's accomplishments include pressuring cosmetic companies not to use animals in testing—an effort that ushered in the recent wave of "cruelty-free" cosmetic products—and stopping General Motors's use of animals in crash tests. PETA activists have

lang supporters attempt to clean derogatory graffiti from Consort's "Home of k.d. lang" sign. Alberta ranchers reacted fiercely to lang's PETA campaign, but many of her fans stood by her. "She hasn't taken away our freedom of choice," they asked, "why should we take away hers?"

disrupted fashion shows worldwide, exposing the cruelty of the fur industry. And the organization has garnered a host of celebrity spokespeople, including musicians Paul McCartney and the B-52's and actors Bea Arthur and Kim Basinger.

Banking on lang's popularity and her upbringing in cattle country to drive home the message of vegetarianism, PETA approached the singer about their "Meat Stinks" campaign idea. lang agreed to film the PSA in Los Angeles at a retirement ranch for old animals, because "I don't believe killing animals for culinary needs is necessary or right." Cuddling a big-eyed cow named Lulu, lang stated her message directly: "We all love animals, but why do we call some 'pets' and some 'dinner'? If you knew how meat was made, you'd probably lose your lunch. I know—I'm from cattle country, and that's why I became a vegetarian. Meat stinks, and not just for animals, but for human health and for the environment."

Before the PSA was to air, it previewed on "Entertainment Tonight," whose crew had been invited along for the filming. The "Meat Stinks" spot immediately set off an explosion that neither PETA nor lang had anticipated. The morning after the "ET" airing, phones at the offices of Warner Brothers Records, PETA, and Larry Wanagas's Bumstead Productions were ringing off the hook. Mail also began flooding the Bumstead office—more than 1,000 negative responses over the next several weeks.

The publicity given the "Meat Stinks" campaign by the "Entertainment Tonight" clip was enough to start an official protest against lang and PETA by cattle and meat industry associations. The president of the National Cattlemen's Association, John Lacey, issued an immediate statement claiming that "there are no credible scientific facts to support the campaign's message that beef is bad for human health and the environment." The North Dakota Beef Commission pronounced on a billboard, "THE WEST WASN'T WON ON SALAD!"

Within days, country radio stations throughout the cattle ranching regions of North America began boycotting lang's records, creating a media blitz that continued for weeks. In Butte, Montana, a radio station program director stated, "If she's going to boycott one of our state's

In recent years PETA has become notorious for media-grabbing animal rights protests, many involving anti-fur celebrities such as talk-show host Ricki Lake and supermodel Cindy Crawford. The militant group rewarded lang for her steadfast support with its Humanitarian Award in 1990.

major industries, we're going to boycott her music." "She is simply involved with a campaign that could destroy some of our listeners' livelihoods," complained another program director in Lexington, Kentucky. Almost three dozen stations followed suit by announcing that they were dropping k.d. lang from their playlists. Some disc jockeys went even further, breaking lang's records on the air or scratching needles across them. How could a country music star criticize the industry that supported many of her listeners?

In western Canada in particular, people felt burned by lang's PETA endorsement. lang's public assertion that "I know—I'm from cattle country, and that's why I became a vegetarian" seemed like a slap in the face to the country that had nurtured her career. The Alberta minister of agriculture, Gordon Mitchell, called lang's decision "extremely unfortunate." "There's a certain feeling of betrayal," he observed to the press. "We have supported k.d. lang fairly well in Alberta."

lang was a favorite in Canada, the first major Canadian country recording star since Anne Murray. Only months before, lang had taped a TV special, "k.d. lang's Buffalo Cafe," on location in Red Deer, where she had spent so much time in the early 1980s. The special featured performances by Dwight Yoakam and Stompin' Tom Connors, a Canadian country music legend. Connors had been semiretired for several years, but the chance to support lang brought him back to the stage. "She's good for Canada," he mused. "Canada needs this kind of shot in the arm." For the occasion, Connors composed a song called "Lady k.d. lang."

Mainstream country artist Dwight Yoakam appeared in "k.d. lang's Buffalo Cafe," a television special that saw lang salute her Canadian roots.

As with *Absolute Torch and Twang,* "Buffalo Cafe" was designed as a sort of tribute to lang's Canadian roots. "This is where I'm from, and this is where I get most of the imagery and visualizations for my music and performance," lang explained about the purpose of filming in Alberta. "It's sort of coming full circle to come back." Later, the special won two Emmy awards for Best Variety Program and Best Variety Performance. But suddenly, with "Meat Stinks," things flip-flopped for lang in Canada—the "Alberta Rose," as she had been proclaimed at the Calgary Olympics just two years before, wilted. "We're getting pretty fed up with these celebrities who think they're experts in areas where they have no expertise," protested the general manager of the Canadian Cattlemen's Association. Several small radio stations in Alberta and the two large country stations in Edmonton and Calgary banned lang's records from their airwaves.

"The vortex of the controversy was in my hometown," lang later remembered. Consort had erected a proud sign on the edge of town that read "Home of k.d. lang." When the "Meat Stinks" controversy hit, vandals defaced the sign with hateful, homophobic graffiti: "EAT BEEF DYKE" was spray-painted across it. When local supporters of lang were unable to clean the vicious slogan from the sign, it was removed from the entrance to town. lang's mother received a flood of hate mail and phone calls. "It was like you'd imagine a TV movie about something hateful in a small town in the South to be," sister Keltie Lang explained. "It wasn't so much the criticism in the press," lang says of the ordeal. "It was the personal attacks on my family that were really painful. Alberta is a small place. Everyone treats you like you're their own. They're your best fans but they're also your worst critics. It can be very double-sided."

Though Larry Wanagas remembers that he "could have filled my trunk with the CDs and cassettes that came back," ultimately, the boycott fell flat—the ruckus stirred up by a few dozen radio stations worked in lang's favor. Over the next few months her record sales quadrupled. "Warner thrived on the publicity," lang states. "At first they thought it might hurt sales. But those men in the trucks out there, those aren't the guys you see at my concerts."

k. d. lang

In fact, many of the radio stations who self-righteously announced they were cutting lang from their playlists were the ones that had never played lang's records in the first place. The lang "boycott" was just one more way to express the homophobia that the vandalizers of the Consort town sign came right out with when they scrawled "EAT BEEF DYKE" across it. A Wichita, Kansas, broadcaster, for example, complained in code that it was not "ladylike" for lang to use her name against the meat industry.

Many other radio stations and journalists came to lang's defense. "She's an unusual person in many respects, but she is a very good singer," said the program director at a Kansas station, whose listeners voted overwhelmingly not to join the boycott.

In *Billboard,* Bill Flanagan, editor of *Musician* magazine, called the boycott nothing less than censorship, a "hunger for publicity" on the part of the stations involved. "Censoring somebody for their ideology is bad enough. But here we're on to something new: censoring somebody for promotional purposes." Flanagan went on to speculate that if radio started censoring other country stars for alcoholism and drug abuse, "There will be a lot of dead air on the radio dial."

Ultimately, one singer denouncing meat was not something a majority of listeners were willing to get excited about. In fact, the beef industry had been struggling with a tarnished image long before lang made her public statement against it. The late 1980s had witnessed a new health consciousness among Americans, brought on by a rise in the rate of heart disease, which was linked by doctors to many factors, including eating red meat. In a series of damage-control commercials, the beef industry hired actor James Garner to tout beef as "Real food for real people"—but then Garner made unwanted headlines by having to undergo bypass surgery for clogged arteries. Another endorser, actor Cybill Shepherd, had lost a lucrative contract for beef commercials when she told a fashion magazine that one of her biggest beauty secrets was not eating meat. When it came down to it, the meat industry was in trouble on its own, without any help from k.d. lang and PETA.

Canadians forgave "the Alberta Rose." "There is talk, among Alberta ranchers," wrote author James Strecker in the *Ottawa Citizen,* "of a lynching substitute—record burnings—to eradicate the offending existence of a pop star who dares to win a Grammy and also reveal an intelligent brain. But k.d. lang is a country-and-western woman star of her own making. . . . In getting palsy with Lulu, Ms. lang is a real, not fake, outlaw."

A few months later, lang was awarded a prestigious honor in her native country when she was named Canada's Female Artist of the Decade at a gala event in Toronto. The award had only been given once before, to Anne Murray for the decade of the 1970s. A board of 75 prominent members of Canada's music industry had chosen lang, also selecting Bryan Adams as Male Artist of the Decade and Rush as Group of the Decade. At the ceremony in November 1989, lang received the award from the presenter of her choice—Margaret Atwood, one of Canada's most renowned fiction writers, who saluted lang by saying, "You can't defy convention, you can't counter tradition. Unless, of course, you're very good. k.d. lang is very good." lang then dedicated her performance of "(Write Me) In Care of the Blues" to her manager, Larry Wanagas.

The "Meat Stinks" controversy was an experience that lang would not forget. It seems to account for much of her reluctance to make a public statement about her homosexuality. It was after the "Meat Stinks" publicity that her mother asked her to promise to be less outspoken and more circumspect on certain issues—including being a lesbian—for fear of hostile repercussions. Having "DYKE" scrawled across her daughter's name must have filled Audrey Lang with fear. And k.d. has never revealed what the hate mail to her mother actually said.

lang admitted an uncertainty about keeping her promise to her mother, because "I'm the kind of person who tends to blurt out what I shouldn't blurt out." But she did tentatively agree to abide by her mother's wishes. The unexpected fury she had felt had made her gun-shy of controversy. "I went from being Canada's little queen," she later observed, "to all of a sudden having the whole country against me. It's a little scary to feel that wave shift." If it had to happen, though, she mused, "I just thank God that it was something I truly believe in."

CHAPTER NINE

CONSTANT
CRAVING

In the shuffle of publicity surrounding k.d. lang's PSA on animal rights, her involvement on behalf of another current social issue was almost overlooked. In early 1990, lang was asked to take part in a video/recording project called *Red Hot + Blue,* the proceeds of which would go toward AIDS research.

Red Hot + Blue would be a compilation of songs by the legendary composer Cole Porter (a closeted gay man), performed in various styles by pop and rock artists and produced as both a record and as a video. The unprecedented project would include such heavy hitters as U2, Erasure, Sinéad O'Connor, The Neville Brothers, Debbie Harry, Iggy Pop, David Byrne, and Annie Lennox performing their interpretations of Porter's songs for the purpose of raising funds for AIDS. The music industry's earlier contribution on behalf of AIDS was the 1986 "That's What Friends Are For," a song composed by Burt Bacharach and Carole Bayer Sager and performed by Dionne Warwick and a host of celebrity friends. The hit single

Transforming herself into a self-styled "post-nuclear cabaret" chanteuse, lang performs "Constant Craving" at the 1993 Grammy Awards. Her album *Ingenue,* with its soulful, jazzy vocals and raw emotions, revealed a different side to the artist.

had raised over $1 million for AIDS research. But *Red Hot + Blue* represented an even more massive, ambitious undertaking, which would not only raise money but teach the public about the epidemic through educational liner notes with sections entitled "What AIDS Is and Isn't" and "What We Can Do About It."

At that time, lang had not personally lost any friends to AIDS, but her belief in the importance of the issue led her to jump at the invitation to be part of *Red Hot + Blue*. The AIDS crisis, lang said, was "mismanaged by the media from the early stages, and I think Christian society has been really irresponsible as well." Coming at a time when lang had hit her head against the country music wall a few too many times, *Red Hot + Blue* gave her a chance to explore a different genre of music—the jazzy, sophisticated torch song.

To direct her video segment, lang sought out the German filmmaker Percy Adlon, whose work she had admired in the quirky movie *Bagdad Cafe*. It was Adlon's idea for lang to do Porter's "So in Love," a masochistic song that foreshadowed lang's next album. "So taunt me and hurt me/deceive me, desert me/I'm yours till I die," Porter's lyrics enjoin. But giving the song a new twist, Adlon filmed lang as an AIDS caregiver, stoically sweating over loads of laundry, then breaking down as she hugs a woman's slip—a touch that lang herself added.

"It's important to me to let people know that women get AIDS too," she explained later, "that it's not just a gay male disease. To me, holding the slip showed how it could be my mother, my aunt, my lover, my sister, it could be me. Women get AIDS." It was a radical move on her part at a time when very few people were paying attention to the fact that women indeed contracted HIV and in increasingly alarming numbers. Mixed in with campy versions of "What a Swell Party This Is" by Debbie Harry and Iggy Pop and "Don't Fence Me In" by David Byrne, which did not speak to the AIDS epidemic at all, the "So in Love" video was inarguably one of the most political contributions to *Red Hot + Blue* and gained kudos from AIDS activists. And to the lesbian and gay community it also looked like a step toward publicly coming out— after all, the slip made it clear that she was singing "So in Love" to a woman.

lang starred as Kotz, a half-Eskimo loner, in the film *Salmonberries*. Director Percy Adlon was so captivated by lang that he created the role for her: "She's one of those personalities who are totally incomparable. . . . a mixture of innocence and slyness. Young, and at the same time wise and old. Both a woman and a man. Tough, and yet very delicate and fragile."

The video led to bigger things. Percy Adlon told one reporter that meeting lang was like being "struck with lightning." In fact, he was so taken with lang after working with her on "So in Love" that he decided to build a feature-length movie around a character written specifically for her. *Salmonberries* was another important step for lang, since the character Adlon wrote for her was clearly a lesbian.

Salmonberries takes place in Kotzebue, Alaska, where a German librarian named Roswitha (played by Adlon's *Bagdad Cafe* star, Rosel Zech) meets her match in a young orphan, also named Kotzebue, or Kotz (lang). Kotz, a half-white, half-Eskimo foundling, is an alienated, gender-bending loner with an explosive undercurrent, who has come to the town she is named for looking for her identity and her birth parents.

Throughout most of the first half of the movie, Kotz barely speaks but is prone to bursting into violent rages in her frustration at not being known or understood. When the librarian continues to mistake her for a boy, Kotz strips naked in the library stacks, and lang has a split-second nude scene, which she was reluctant to do. "k.d. thought she was too clumsy and big [for the scene]," Adlon remembers. "I said to her, 'Haven't you ever looked at Greek and Roman sculptures? These ladies are all pretty big and wonderful. I like you how you are.' She didn't believe it and did some fasting—I think it was more mental fasting—and prepared herself spiritually." In retrospect, lang decided that the brief nude scene "was a beautiful way to deal with things, because I have been called 'sir' so many times in my life and will always be."

The character Roswitha, adrift from her country and her family since her husband was killed trying to escape East Berlin in the 1960s, is a different kind of outsider. Through Kotz's persistence, the two women form a bond of friendship across age and culture; but to Kotz's disappointment, Roswitha does not want the relationship to become a physical one. Against the background of endless snow and ice, lang's clear voice sings "Barefoot," the song she wrote for the movie. "I'd walk through the snow barefoot/If you'd open up your door," she begs, then cries a haunting, lonely wolf howl.

Salmonberries are the beautiful red fruit Roswitha has been canning for 20 years and displaying in stacks of jars in her bedroom like beautiful stained glass walls. When Kotz eats berries from an old jar, she finds they have turned to a powerful liqueur that intoxicates her. The berries represent a bottling-up of unfulfilled desires and emotions that surround the librarian like a protective wall, and that inebriate the younger woman Kotz.

The movie was filmed in Alaska in late 1990 and Berlin in early 1991, after the collapse of the Berlin Wall. Adlon used the reunification of Germany as "a political subtext . . . to a movie about breaking down barriers at a personal level." Location filming in Alaska was brutal, with lang coming close to frostbite on her nose when she was exposed to the arctic temperatures. Adlon remembers lang's fury when a scene called for costar Rosel Zech to walk barefoot through the snow. After shooting, "k.d. rubbed and kissed Rosel's feet, like a bear mother protecting her baby."

Though lang's acting in *Salmonberries* is often stilted, Rosel Zech delivers a memorable performance, and the film manages to be a thoughtful love story about people building walls around themselves, then finding ways to reach through them to connect to others. Unfortunately, *Salmonberries* never saw major theatrical release. It had a test screening at the New York Gay and Lesbian Film Festival, where *Village Voice* columnist Michael Musto described it as provoking "a near riot." "The queer crowd," wrote Musto, "was frustrated that the tease [when Kotz tries to have sex with Roswitha] didn't seem to be going any further, while the straights seemed horrified that the tease was there at all."

Every major distributor, according to Adlon, passed on the chance to bring it to North American audiences. *Salmonberries* made the rounds of film festivals and won the Best Film category at the renowned Montreal World Film Festival in September 1991. A limited video distribution made it accessible to the very few who could afford the $69.95 price tag. Not surprisingly, the video showed up in many lesbian bookstores and mail-order catalogs, and it was available through lang's fan club. Finally, in 1994, *Salmonberries* had a brief theatrical release and was subsequently widely distributed on video.

Though she probably didn't realize it, lang's work on *Red Hot + Blue* and *Salmonberries* had paved the way for the next step in her career—a break with country music and a turn toward a new style of singing and songwriting.

For a while, lang had been setting up her fans and the public for her ultimate break with country music. Around the time that *Absolute Torch and Twang* was released, lang told a *New York Times* reporter, "It's becoming less and less clear to me where I fit in with Nashville. While I respect its role in the history of country music, I don't want to be thought of solely as a country artist. I prefer to be user friendly with Nashville. Hopefully, they'll respect what I do, and our paths will collide once in a while." Asked for examples of singers who were "user friendly" with Nashville, lang cited Ray Charles and Roy Orbison.

Filming *Salmonberries* allowed lang to take a much-needed break from what she called the endless cycle of "making records and touring, making records and touring nonstop." But it was while on location for the film that lang came up with the concept for her next album, which she decided to title *Ingenue* before she had even written a note of music or a single lyric. "Ingenue," lang defines, "means unworldly, naive, artless. An unworldly artless woman played by an actress." She has repeatedly called it her most personal album to date. "The writing is totally autobiographical, naked, and real—if I was toothpaste and you squeezed me, you'd get *Ingenue*," she contends.

During the break between filming *Salmonberries* in Alaska and then in Germany and Poland, lang and Ben Mink went to work writing *Ingenue*. To begin, Mink says they locked themselves "in a room like two monkeys and we set up a trapeze of instruments. . . . Maybe a pot will fall on the floor and make a musical note. Anything can go into the mix." Mink's description of their collaborative style sounded oddly reminiscent of lang's early work with her friend Drifter.

Breaking out of the country music genre freed lang and Mink from having to use standard instruments, and both found the prospect of

Kotz and German émigré Roswitha (Rosel Zech) embrace in *Salmonberries*. The independent film focuses on the bonds and boundaries between two outsiders in a tentative lesbian relationship.

incorporating other musical influences into their compositions very exciting. They scattered traces of Indian melodies and bits of music from Mink's Hasidic culture throughout the album and constantly searched for new sounds to incorporate. "Even during the middle of the writing process we didn't know exactly what was happening," lang says. "We'd get glimpses of what we were doing, but it was never full focus, and we'd just keep creating these sounds and these pieces."

Country metaphors were likewise liberated from lang's lyrics. The result is that the songs have all of the torch her fans were familiar with, but none of the same twang of her country compositions. Song titles like "Save Me," "Wash Me Clean," "Still Thrives This Love," "Season of Hollow Soul," "Tears of Love's Recall," and "Constant Craving" indicate the thematic angle of the album. "Pain creates great art," lang explained of the yearning and longing that laces through the songs. "There's nothing like a good heartbreak to get a good song." In fact, lang later admitted that she wrote *Ingenue* while recovering from unrequited love; when she publicly came out, she confessed that the object of her passion had been a woman. Life, it seems, does imitate art: the heartbreak of the character Kotz had become lang's own.

"I was definitely a stalker," lang mused later of her painful love addiction. "Obsession is a weird thing, like an unhealthy sort of exercise. *Ingenue* was this great work of art, this great gift, this great gesture: You see, I'm really in love with you, look what I've done. Now that it's basically over, it's sort of going: No, it's yours, Kathryn, it's yours. You wrote it, you sang it, it's your record, not hers."

The deeply personal side of *Ingenue* was difficult for lang, writing and singing lyrics that ripped her heart and soul open for the world to see. Each take during the recording sessions was emotionally and physically draining. She was having problems with her pitch, which had never troubled her before, and worried that she was losing her gift. "I was singing from the pain of the writer," she later told Ann Magnuson in *Elle* magazine, "and, technically, it made my pitch flat. . . . I went through an emotional breakdown. I had to go through therapy, where I realized that I was singing from the pain."

In addition to the emotional trauma she was experiencing, there was a physiological reason behind the problem: lang was in need of a root canal. Traveling to Europe to film the last part of *Salmonberries,* lang underwent extensive dental work and spent much time alone before resuming the recording of *Ingenue.* "Traveling renews you," she told Liza Minnelli in *Interview* magazine. "In fact, my trip to Poland made me feel born again. Not that fame has been an overwhelming thing in my life, but it was great just going someplace where no one cares who the hell you are and you don't care who the hell you are."

During the time she was working on *Ingenue,* lang stopped listening to country music and studied pop and jazz singers—Karen Carpenter, Carmen McRae, Peggy Lee, Julie London, and Billie Holiday. It was not bitterness with the country music establishment, she insisted, that determined the shift. "What made me change was that I wanted to explore the different personalities within my music," lang says. She had, in fact, told Larry Wanagas when he first became her manager that she wanted to be a jazz singer, and with songs like "Black Coffee" on *Shadowland* and "So in Love" on *Red Hot + Blue* she had been edging further into that arena.

And lang was also getting older; she turned 30 alone in Paris in November 1991 while on a promotional tour for *Salmonberries.* She later called *Ingenue* part of having reached her "Saturn return," a period between the ages of 28 and 31 that is "basically a change in people's attitudes and a big turning point in their lives." lang found that the influences of her early youth—Broadway musicals, film scores, and classical music—were shifting to the surface of her music. Her song "Constant Craving" seemed to speak to lang's desire to develop and fulfill herself as an artist: "Maybe a great magnet pulls/All souls toward truth/Or maybe it is life itself/That feeds wisdom to its youth."

Ingenue was released in March 1992. Notably absent from the album was her band, the reclines. "The reclines had developed a certain sound," lang explained about the breakup of the band. "It was a country sound." Even the album cover had a new look, with soft, sepia-toned photographs of lang in an apparent state of angst. Interviewers barraged lang with questions about her switch from country music to what she termed "post-nuclear cabaret"—as if performers should not explore different forms and genres if they want and need to. "I certainly am a person who lives by the rule that change is the essence of growth," lang answered one reporter. "Change is what fuels me. . . . I had been as creative as possible with country music. . . . It's like a lover that it's time to leave."

"Lush and luscious," Joe Brown proclaimed the album in the *Washington Post,* with "creamy, croony vocals." "The songs proceed from infatuation to disappointment to survival with a cohesive richness of tone and sensibility," Stacey D'Erasmo wrote in the *Village Voice.* "There are no throwaways here."

But many reviewers found lang's shift from energetic country to "sappy" lounge music disheartening. The yearning of the songs was, in fact, relentless. Stephanie Zacharek in *Entertainment Weekly* labeled *Ingenue* "a drastic departure" that marked "a plummet in energy." "The listener," Zacharek complained, "feels like a bedmate who . . . can muster only enough enthusiasm to open one eye and roll over." Likewise, Ralph Novak wrote in *People* magazine that the album was "ennuyeuse" (boring). Easy listening music about a hopeless, almost masochistic love was not what many had expected—or wanted—from k.d. lang.

Yet lang remained convinced about the strength and importance of her material. "There's only one subject to talk about, really," she concluded, waxing wistful on the topic of love. "It's certainly the only thing to write about."

Almost immediately, speculation started about who had been the focus of lang's unrequited love—who could have instilled so much melancholy and "constant craving" in cowgirl k.d. lang? lang remained close-lipped about both the name and the gender of her paramour. "My private life belongs to me," she stated unequivocally.

But just as lang got ready to embark on her grueling 100-city tour to promote *Ingenue,* the gay magazine the *Advocate* came knocking on her door. Still in the middle of her "Saturn return," lang had one more turning point in front of her.

CHAPTER TEN

THINGS THAT
I MAY TELL YOU

Nineteen ninety-two would be a hopeful but wary year for lesbians and gay men after over a decade of sadness, anger, and frustration. Sadness at the loss of so many thousands to AIDS. Anger at two Republican administrations' homophobic foot-dragging approach to combating the epidemic. And frustration at being consistently misrepresented and demonized—when represented at all—in popular culture and the media.

What had emerged from a decade of hard knocks was a lesbian and gay community fiercely determined to take care of its own, with a renewed commitment to fighting. The Stonewall Rebellion of 1969 in New York City—when a group of drag queens, neighborhood gay people, and street kids rioted to oppose police harassment of a New York City gay bar—had shown the world what could happen when gay people had had enough of being victimized. And Stonewall had taught gay people that being silent and closeted

lang strides confidently to center stage. In *Finding Her Voice,* Mary Bufwack and Robert Oermann report that eight other prominent women in country music history are alleged to be gay, but lang is the first singer to be so open and forthright.

just would not cut it when their rights and dignity were being stripped away and their lives were on the line.

In the mid- and late 1980s, while the AIDS epidemic raged on, lesbian and gay activists shored themselves up through the creation of community centers, safe places where lesbian and gay organizing could flourish. The chief direct-action groups of the 1980s, AIDS Coalition to Unleash Power (ACT UP), Queer Nation, and the media watchdog Gay and Lesbian Alliance Against Defamation (GLAAD), were all born at public forums at New York's Lesbian and Gay Community Services Center. Key slogans were "Silence = Death" and "We're here, we're queer, get used to it!" which denoted the increasingly feisty, fed-up stance of much of the lesbian and gay liberation movement.

The techniques used by queer activists to drive their points home to city hall, to Washington, and to Hollywood were often spectacular and media-grabbing "zaps." ACT UP–ers lay down in the middle aisle of New York's St. Patrick's Cathedral during a mass to protest the Catholic Church's pernicious views on homosexuality and on AIDS education in the schools. The Marys, a subgroup of ACT UP, staged public funerals for those who died of AIDS, carrying their friends' coffins through the streets of New York and Washington to illustrate the pointless suffering and death that the government had allowed to happen. GLAAD picketed Hollywood studios and barraged them with mail protesting offensive films like *Silence of the Lambs,* whose villain was yet another crazed transvestite mass murderer, and *Basic Instinct,* whose rare lesbian/bisexual lead character preyed on unsuspecting straight men with an icepick.

Less radical lesbian and gay organizers took the route of electoral politics, registering massive numbers of lesbian and gay voters to try to solidify a "gay vote" and helping to raise money for candidates who seemed sympathetic, most notably Bill Clinton in 1992. Candidate Clinton promised in return to pay close attention to the AIDS epidemic by appointing an "AIDS czar" and to lift the ban that Ronald Reagan had imposed on gays in the military. When Clinton won his party's nomination he made the unprecedented move of advocating gay rights from the podium of the Democratic National Convention. To many gay people, the prospect of a pro-gay Democratic president after 12 years of Republican reaction seemed like a dream come true.

It is no surprise that the two sides of the gay-activism coin—"let's work within the system" and "let's turn the system upside down"—were often at loggerheads over which techniques were most capable of effecting change. And they sometimes came to blows over one of the most controversial of the queer radicals' tactics—"outing." For radical activists, electoral politics alone would not save the thousands who were going to die of AIDS; a revolution was necessary. It was in a climate of frustration and aggressive activism that outing was first employed, and it was the gay magazine *OutWeek* that brought it to national prominence.

OutWeek magazine was founded in New York City in 1989 by ACT UP members Gabriel Rotello and Michaelangelo Signorile. Funded by a wealthy gay businessman with AIDS, *OutWeek* was designed as a publication that would push people's buttons and serve as a forum for ACT UP's views. The magazine very quickly gained a reputation for what Signorile has called "in-your-face journalism." The particular technique that propelled *OutWeek* and Signorile to national attention was dubbed by *Time* magazine as "outing."

Outing, as explained by Gabriel Rotello, is the practice of "equalizing homosexuality and heterosexuality in the media." Signorile outlined the function of outing in his book *Queer in America: Sex, the Media, and the Closets of Power:*

> Whenever it's pertinent, a public figure's homosexuality should be discussed and inquired about. This should be true only for public figures — rich and famous individuals who've made a deal with the public: In return for the millions of dollars they earn and/or the power they wield, their lives are open for dissection by the media. . . . By not reporting about famous gays, the message the media send is clear: Homosexuality is so utterly grotesque that it should never be discussed.

Local chapters of ACT UP had outed public officials such as Oregon Senator Mark Hatfield, whose record of voting against AIDS funding was actively killing gay people. After the senator's campaign billboards were spray-painted to read "CLOSETED GAY: LIVING A LIE, VOTING TO OPPRESS," Hatfield's voting record improved dramatically.

Signorile's outing of billionaire publisher Malcolm Forbes in March of 1990—shortly after Forbes died—made national headlines, commented on by such mainstream organs as the *New York Times, USA Today,* and *Playboy.* The mainstream press—and many conservative gay activists—viewed Signorile's outing of Forbes as "fascism," a terrorist tactic right out of Joseph McCarthy's Communist witch-hunts of the 1950s. Dragging someone unwillingly out of the closet, the mainstream media argued, was an "invasion of privacy" that would never achieve the goal of creating gay role models. But, Signorile countered, outing did not discuss sex acts, which were private; it discussed sexual orientation and identity, which were, or should be, public. And it did not seek to produce a legion of role models; instead, it was creating much-needed visibility. Signorile's column in *OutWeek,* called "Gossip Watch," became a must-read for the lesbian and gay community as well as for straight media, as the indignant reporter screamed at closeted public figures in capital letters: "SOMETHING HAS TO BE DONE AND IT HAS TO BE DONE FAST. AND YOU ARE IN POSITIONS TO DO IT."

Other publications and activists also began employing outing. In the pages of the *Advocate* in 1991, Signorile outed Department of Defense official Pete Williams for hypocritical obeisance to the military's policy against gay servicepeople. That same year, a group of New York activists, calling themselves OutPost, began a campaign of plastering posters of Hollywood celebrities like actor Jodie Foster on New York street signs, mailboxes, and lampposts with the slogan "ABSOLUTELY QUEER" on them.

For Signorile and others who regularly exposed gay public figures, outing was a natural outgrowth of the new militant queer activism. It was vital to lesbian and gay survival for both the straight and gay communities to know just how many gay people there were in the country and the world. "Kids should know who's gay regardless of whether the people are proper role models," Signorile wrote. "Eddie Murphy isn't necessarily the greatest role model, but it's important for black youth that a top box-office star is black." Given the statistics that lesbian and gay youth are at higher risk for suicide, alcoholism, drug abuse, and HIV infection than heterosexual teens, Signorile's argument became a particularly critical one.

In the spring of 1992 *OutWeek* magazine ceased publication due to financial troubles, and the main conduit for lesbian and gay news and views became the Los Angeles–based *Advocate*. The *Advocate* had been in existence since 1967 but was predominantly known as a men's magazine with a hot-and-heavy personals section and explicit phone sex ads that could bring a blush to many cheeks. By the early 1990s the

Demonstrators demand increased effort to find a cure for AIDS. Though lang has been involved with many AIDS benefit projects, she has consistently reiterated her desire to be viewed as a musician first and foremost, not a political activist.

magazine was making an attempt to become a more serious news vehicle and to attract more women readers, and it added some prominent lesbian journalists to its staff roster. It was also in search of a new, more mainstream look, a glossy face that would make it the gay equivalent of *Time* or *Newsweek*.

The *Advocate* had tried to interview k.d. lang several times over the years, but always with no luck. lang and her handlers were well aware what the magazine was after—a splashy public coming-out. When the *Advocate* decided to switch to high-gloss in mid-1992, the editors searched for an enticing cover story that would attract readers to the magazine's new image. So, once again, they called on k.d. lang.

While she hadn't denied anything—and had by 1992 appeared as a lesbian in a music video and a feature film—lang had effectively sidestepped the question of her sexual orientation in more than one interview. Her roughest time—but perhaps strongest moment—had been handling interviewer Connie Chung, who in 1989 had baited lang on national television.

"Are you in love now?" Chung asked.

"Yeah," lang answered shyly.

"Somebody back home?"

"Yeah."

"I want to ask," Chung said coyly, "marriage?"

"No."

"Why not?" Chung pursued, not giving up despite the one-word replies.

"It's just not important. A piece of paper doesn't mean anything to me. Let's change the subject." And lang closed the door.

But how long could she continue to "not deny"? lang later claimed that she was not annoyed with Chung's tenacious line of questioning but stated wearily, "I get a little tired of the issue, because ultimately I'm a musician."

The "I'm an artist, not an activist" line has grated on a lot of nerves in the lesbian and gay political arena. Though lang insisted that sexual orientation had nothing to do with art, she had encountered an enormous amount of implicit and explicit homophobia during her

Looking dapper at the 1993 American Music Awards, lang jubilantly accepts the award for Best New Female Adult Contemporary Artist. After nearly a decade in country music, lang finally reaped major rewards in the pop genre.

career. "It's not enough to be an artist," writer Paul Monette has said. "If you live in cataclysmic times, if the lightning rod of history strikes you, then all art is political, and all art that is not consciously so still partakes of the politics, if only to run away."

lang's fears must have included being pigeonholed as part of the "women's music" movement, a categorization she had always resisted. The women's music industry was an outgrowth of lesbian-feminist activism of the early 1970s. Since lesbians were invisible in mainstream culture, they sought to create for themselves positive images of their lives, hopes, and dreams. Singers such as Holly Near, Cris Williamson, and Meg Christian, whose musical influences came out of the American folk tradition, sang about female lovers, crushes on gym teachers, and a vast (though at that time mostly white) "lesbian nation."

Holly Near had come closest to having a mainstream career, after she teamed up with folk legend Ronnie Gilbert of the 1950s group the Weavers; but she never achieved major recognition. All of the other "stars" of the women's music industry were confined to limited recognition and record sales, though their support at lesbian music festivals and concerts was strong.

k.d. lang belonged to another group of female musicians. The trail was blazed, critic Arlene Stein points out, by singers Madonna and Cyndi Lauper, who pushed the limits of what was "acceptable" for women performers and proved that they could indeed sell records, and lots of them. Then came k.d. lang, Tracy Chapman, Michelle Shocked, and Melissa Etheridge singing gutsy, gender-free lyrics that could appeal to either sex. Lesbian fans couldn't get enough of them. Young women who had never thought of themselves as feminists rushed to buy their records and go to their concerts. But the careers of these stars were not dependent on gigs at lesbian music festivals. And though they were all reportedly gay, none of them had made an official statement.

lang preferred to keep things open for herself and not to be labeled. "Androgyny to me," lang said, "is making your sexuality available, through your art, to everyone. Like Elvis, like Mick Jagger, like Annie Lennox or Marlene Dietrich—using the power of both male and female."

Only the rock group Two Nice Girls was at that time completely out of the closet. Gretchen Phillips, a member of the band, recalls that when they first negotiated with Rough Trade, their recording company, they said, "We're going to be really out. Do you have any problem with that?" But Two Nice Girls, though very successful, has never achieved the fame of k.d. lang or Melissa Etheridge.

By 1992 lang felt pretty secure in her career. Unlike Two Nice Girls, her name was a household word. She had weathered the "Meat Stinks" controversy and sold more records than ever. She had won two Grammy awards and had a hit record climbing the pop charts ("Constant Craving"). She had stood up to the country music establishment and then dropped quietly into another genre. She had starred in a film as a lesbian. And then there was the "Saturn return," the time of momentous change in a person's life. Many factors came together at just that moment in 1992 to affect lang's decision to do more than "not deny."

And this time, when the *Advocate* called, she said yes.

Brendan Lemon is an editor at the *New Yorker* magazine who also often writes features for the gay press. The *Advocate* editors pegged him to do the lang interview in London, where she was kicking off her *Ingenue* tour. Clearly, lang was ambivalent about the interview; Lemon had only a few hours' notice to get on a plane for England. It would be on lang's terms or not at all. But if she acted like a diva in setting up the interview, lang displayed what Lemon called "pure country-bred gallantry" once he arrived in London. The interview got off to a slow start, but built to a climax in which lang didn't so much walk out of the closet on her own as let Lemon lead her out by the hand.

"I don't feel political about my preference," lang insisted, getting riled when Lemon started steering her toward a discussion of sexuality. "I just don't. I'm sorry! I'm sorry to disappoint you hard-cores, but I don't! . . . It certainly isn't my cause. But I also have never denied it. I don't try to hide it like some people in the industry do."

"But there's a difference," Lemon pursued gently, "between not denying it and finally just saying 'I'm a lesbian.' That's the difference."

"Yeah, it's a difference," lang agreed.

k. d. lang

lang basks in the glow of greater acclaim and a new level of stardom. Contrary to conventional wisdom, lang's open homosexuality did not impact negatively on her career: "Coming out was totally positive—like an emotional veil had been lifted and taken away."

"And what do you have to lose at this point?" Lemon wondered. "There's going to be a point at which you just don't want to hedge any more and you say, 'Let me come out and then go on with my life as an artist.'"

"Well," lang said, "I think I'm at that point."

And there it was, a tentative admission, but the impact of it would be as strong as if she had grabbed the tape recorder and shouted into it, "I'm a lesbian!"

Lemon then engaged lang in a more open discussion about why she had not spoken up about her sexual orientation, and lang revealed her promise to her mother. "Man, if I didn't worry about my mother, I'd be the biggest parader in the whole world," lang said. But she concluded, "I think my mother's proud of me for being an individual and being brave enough to talk about it."

After the interview, lang called up her manager and her publicist and announced, "I think I just came out to the *Advocate*." And then they all waited for the other shoe to drop.

But, in fact, it never did. "When she came out," Larry Wanagas remembers, "there was not a phone call, not a letter; somebody sent back one of her records, and that was it. I think it was a huge weight off her shoulders. She felt completely emancipated."

Sales of her new album skyrocketed. *Ingenue* went platinum in the United States, double platinum in Canada, and gold in Britain and Australia. "Constant Craving" stayed in the pop charts for six months, rising all the way to the top. At the Grammy Awards lang took home the honor for Best Female Pop Vocalist, and at the American Music Awards she was voted Best New Female Adult Contemporary Artist. When approached by the press backstage after the AMA honor with the question, "How do you feel?" lang quipped, "I feel adult. I feel contemporary. And I feel new."

"It signals a whole new era of possibilities for celebrities," Torie Osborn, former executive director of the National Gay and Lesbian Task Force said of lang's coming-out. "The classic thing about celebrities is that they supposedly have so much to lose. . . . She's come out with grace and ease—and no loss in sales."

It was definitely a banner year for k.d. lang to be out as a lesbian, but she knew that she had been extraordinarily lucky that the tenor of the times was in her favor. "As a gay woman I would love to see homophobia dissipated," she told *Interview* magazine at the end of 1992. "We've come a long way, but the pendulum will constantly swing back and forth."

JUST KEEP ME
MOVING

There is a completely different feeling to the interviews that k.d. lang granted to reporters after she came out as a lesbian in June of 1992. In the conversations, she does, in fact, seem "new." About a year after the *Advocate* interview, lang posed for the cover of *Vanity Fair* magazine in a send up of a Norman Rockwell painting; the magazine is now a collector's item. In full male drag, lang sits in a barber chair with her face lathered with shaving cream while supermodel Cindy Crawford, in a scanty leotard, shaves her with a straight razor. Inside, another photo of the two shows "barber" Crawford bending over lang in a blatantly sexual pose, with a caption that reads, "Acting up in a dream-date fantasy, k.d. lang checks out the curves on supermodel Cindy Crawford." The idea of being shaved was lang's idea, while gay photographer Herb Ritts suggested using Cindy Crawford. Though she has repeatedly identified herself as heterosexual,

At the height of her fame, lang remains down-to-earth and focused on what is important to her. "I want to feed the muses," she philosophizes, "to sustain the reciprocity between me and what makes me an artist."

k. d. lang

Crawford's sexual orientation (along with that of her estranged husband, actor Richard Gere) has often been questioned by the media, and the irony of her pairing with the openly lesbian lang was not lost on gay America.

In the accompanying interview with Leslie Bennetts, lang was more straightforward than she had ever been, honestly discussing her recent attempts to understand herself and her problems with intimacy through psychotherapy. Gone was the need to hide, to divert attention from her sexuality with yes and no answers to leading questions or through artful gender-free remarks. "I don't know why I'm gay," she could muse openly in *Vanity Fair*. "I find women more enticing, both emotionally and sexually." It was a long way from the Connie Chung interview!

The same month, on her farm outside Vancouver, British Columbia, lang gave an interview to Mim Udovitch of *Rolling Stone* magazine. Having recently wrapped up her *Ingenue* tour, lang commented on the positive effect coming out had had on her concerts. "The really, really big thing I experienced this year was the intimacy between me and the audience," she noted, "not just because of the number of women, although that's part of it. It's that I feel comfortable knowing that they came there knowing. That I don't have to worry that if they finally figured it out, they would get up and leave." This is a fear, lang conceded, that most gay performers face. "Being out is just great," she said. "I recommend it to people who are ready to do it. Just do it."

In fact, the years 1992 to 1994 saw a record number of major celebrities coming out of the closet. Tennis champion Martina Navratilova; singers Melissa Etheridge, Elton John, and Boy George; actors Rupert Everett, Amanda Bearse, and Dick Sargent—all came out with little public fanfare and much admiration. What was even more significant was that a number of these stars threw themselves wholeheartedly into the struggle for lesbian and gay civil rights and into the fight against AIDS. Martina Navratilova has become one of the gay movement's most vibrant celebrity activists. "I had really felt alienated from the United States of Ronald Reagan and George Bush," says the tennis star, who was born and raised in Czechoslovakia but is now a U.S. citizen. "The gay movement made me feel like I do belong."

Since coming out, k.d. lang has increased her efforts on behalf of the AIDS fight. In her fan club newsletter she encourages fans to find out about local AIDS organizations and to support them. Selective about the benefits she does because "you just can't do them all," lang figures that some days her manager may receive over a dozen requests for her to appear at fund-raisers.

Notable among her AIDS benefit appearances was the Concert of Hope in London, organized by singer George Michael for World AIDS Day in 1992. At a packed Wembley Stadium, with the Princess of Wales in attendance, David Bowie introduced lang as "one of the classiest and most stylish performers of the nineties." lang won over the crowd with "Constant Craving," "Just Keep Me Moving," and "Lifted By Love." "I know the threat of AIDS is a reality and an immense threatening obstacle that we must overcome," she told the audience. "There is only one way we can do that—and that is with love and hope." She dedicated her final song, "Crying," to those living with HIV and received an emotional, enthusiastic standing ovation.

In 1994, lang did back-to-back performances for AIDS, first at the AIDS Project L.A. benefit hosted by gay designer Isaac Mizrahi, and then at LifeBeat in New York during Gay Pride Week with Melissa Etheridge, John Secada, and Queen Latifah. The concert program was so packed with performers that lang didn't begin singing until after one o'clock in the morning; and in her true comic style she showed up on stage in her pajamas. After singing the sixties pop tune "What's New, Pussycat?" and several of her own standards, lang called her good friend Melissa Etheridge onto the stage for a sensual lesbian duet, "You Can Sleep While I Drive," that the audience would not soon forget.

After finishing her *Ingenue* tour, lang's main project was completing the soundtrack to gay filmmaker Gus Van Sant's movie *Even Cowgirls Get the Blues,* based on the cult novel by Tom Robbins about a lesbian hitchhiker. The movie was slated for fall 1993 release but was delayed for six months for lang's sound track, another collaboration with Ben Mink.

"The novel takes place in 1973," explains Mink, "so a lot of the music is sort of period-influenced. We had one day when we did a polka, a jazz-fusion tune, a country waltz, and a Sly and the Family Stone boogie number." lang was matching the mood of the movie and not trying to create a coherent whole, which had made her earlier albums so memorable. And the lack of focus in *Cowgirls* showed through clearly. As one reviewer noted, "The only element tying it together is lang's artistic ambition. . . . Since her loyalties extend only to her voice and her sensibility, the entire world of music remains open to her." The album produced two hit singles, "Lifted By Love" and "Hush Sweet Lover," but on the whole received a lukewarm reception in the press.

In late 1994 lang and Mink began work on their newest album, *all you can eat,* released in the fall of 1995. The album is, lang claims, "more celebrational" than *Ingenue,* which she calls "cathartic." She is conscious of having wanted *all you can eat* to be very different from *Ingenue,* which garnered a host of recognition and awards and which it might be tempting to try to recreate. "It's very hard to stay away from formulation," she admits, "when there's so much pressure to make the money while you're hot. I'm not interested in producing for success. I don't think I'm ever going to be selling forty-two million records. My legend isn't going to be based on sales, but hopefully on the longevity and the purity of the product—on being unique and doing it my way." It appears that she has realized her goal: an early review in the *Advocate* called *all you can eat* "a subtle but immensely substantial work from an artist who refuses to stop evolving for the sake of commercial security."

The album was the first recorded in the new studio lang built for herself on her Vancouver farm, where she lives most of the year with her older sister Keltie, who is also a lesbian, and a menagerie of animals, including goats, horses, dogs, cats, and a pig. It is the kind of place lang has always wanted to own, but which she has never really gotten around to decorating or making "homey." The same is true of the yellow bungalow she rents for part of the year in the Hollywood Hills of Los Angeles. "I get itchy if I'm in one place too long," she explains about her lack of furniture, possessions, and creature comforts. "I don't really feel like I'm ever home anywhere."

The enormous success of *Ingenue* brought fame to lang, but also introduced her to the excesses of being a celebrity. "All my life," she

Unwinding from a busy performing career, lang enjoys watching a tennis match. Having turned the corner of her "Saturn return," lang feels ready to create more "celebrational" music and embraces a state of constant personal and artistic change.

revealed in a recent interview with *Out* magazine, "I've known I would be and wanted to be famous, to have a hit record . . . and with *Ingenue* I got it."

"The high is fantastic," she continues. "But then there's the down, and then there's the vacuum that you enter that makes you want it more. You start to believe the hype." Her new album reflects her focus on self-love, says lang, on a rediscovered sense of who she is and where she comes from. Its style is less orchestrally lush than that of *Ingenue*, more pared down—and more irreverent.

These days lang leads a quiet, unpretentious life, unlike many other celebrities. "I do things simple compared to the way some entertainers live," lang points out. "Once or twice a year, I dress up and do something glamorous, but generally, I don't like night life. I'd rather stay home and cook and then go for a walk." Her sister Keltie affectionately describes her as a "geek." More and more, lang spends time with friends such as Martina Navratilova, who shares lang's love of sports and motorcycles and also understands the rewards and the hazards of being famous. Both lang and her intimate circle of friends and colleagues adamantly refuse to discuss her private life beyond the bare essentials, and the names of women she is dating are strictly off limits, though often hinted at in the gay press.

While lang is at work on a new album, most days are routine. She gets up at seven o'clock in the morning, drinks a protein shake before working out in her home gym, then takes the rest of the morning to fix up the studio, getting it ready for recording. The afternoon is spent at Ben Mink's house, writing the melodies for the album. "I'm really particular about melody," lang notes. Later, after the tunes are composed, lang will tackle the lyrics on her own ("I go off into lyric-land," as she puts it) while Mink works on the chords. "When the studio gets running," lang points out, "we'll be at it eighteen hours a day. It will be inspirational."

lang says that she enjoys hard work and the challenges that touring and recording bring, but that she is in no hurry to become so famous that she is just "going through the motions." The only pressure she feels is an internal one that most artists experience—the need to create. "No one's making you do that," she explains of the creative process. "That is a gift—or a punishment," she adds with a laugh.

"One of my goals is to keep dissatisfied," lang says of her career. Though music is her first love, she would like to move in other directions as well, particularly toward acting in movies or plays. She recently played a born-again Christian in her friend Julie Cypher's film, *Teresa's Tattoo*. In an interview a few years ago, lang outlined a list of other fantasies: "I'd like to be a farmer. I'd like to be an actress, a painter, a motorcycle mechanic. I dream every night that I play [hockey] for the Edmonton Oilers."

k.d. lang is a person who is constantly craving new ideas, inspiration, and artistic direction. "I get glimpses of things I want to do that don't happen for a long time," she told *Rolling Stone*. "That rockabilly rebel is still there, she's still inside, and it's like at the same time you're driving forward, you're waving goodbye, kinda unwillingly. . . . I'm changing all the time. Someone remarked to me just the other day: 'Champions adjust.' So anything could happen."

DISCOGRAPHY

ALBUMS

A Truly Western Experience (Bumstead Productions, 1984)

Angel with a Lariat (Sire Records, 1987)

Shadowland: The Owen Bradley Sessions (Sire Records, 1988)

Absolute Torch and Twang (Sire Records, 1989)

Ingenue (Sire Records, 1992)

Even Cowgirls Get the Blues (Sire Records, 1993)

all you can eat (Warner Brothers, 1995)

COMPILATIONS

Take 6, "Our Day Will Come," from the movie *Shag* (Sire Records, 1989)

Take 6, "Riding the Rails," from the movie *Dick Tracy* (Sire Records, 1990)

"So in Love," *Red Hot + Blue* (Chrysalis, 1990)

"Calling All Angels," with Jane Siberry, from the movie *Until the End of the World* (Warner Brothers, 1991)

"Barefoot," from the movie *Salmonberries—MTV Unplugged, Volume I* (Warner Brothers, 1994)

COLLABORATIONS

Loretta Lynn, Kitty Wells, and Brenda Lee, "Honky Tonk Angels' Medley," *Shadowland* (Sire Records, 1988)

Dwight Yoakam, "Sin City," *Just Looking for a Hit* (Reprise, 1989)

Wendy & Lisa, "Mother of Pearl," *Eroica* (Virgin, 1990)

Roy Orbison, "Crying," *King of Hearts* (Warner Brothers, 1992)

Andy Bell, "No More Tears (Enough Is Enough)," *Coneheads* (Warner Brothers, 1993)

Jane Siberry, "Calling All Angels," *When I Was a Boy* (Sire Records, 1993)

MUSIC VIDEOS

Red Hot + Blue (Chrysalis, 1991)

Harvest of Seven Years (Cropped and Chronicled) (Sire Records, 1992)

CHRONOLOGY

1961   Born Kathryn Dawn Lang on November 2 in
        Edmonton, Canada

1975   Composes her first song, "Hoping My Dreams
        Come True"

1977   Gives her first paid performance, at the Consort
        Kinsmen Club

1978   Reveals her sexual orientation to her mother

1979   Writes and performs her high school graduation
        theme song, "The End of Our Beginning"; enrolls at
        Red Deer College

1981   Becomes a vegetarian; drops out of college and moves
        to Edmonton; opens for country singer Holly Wright

1982   Portrays a Patsy Cline–like character in an Edmonton
        production of *Country Chorale*; auditions for singing
        parts with bands and in radio commercials

1983   Hires Larry Wanagas as manager; chooses country
        music as her style and selects a band, the reclines;
        adopts stage name "k.d. lang"

1984   Writes and records her first single, "Friday Dance
        Promenade"; performs on Canadian country music
        TV show "Sun Country"; cuts her first album, *A
        Truly Western Experience*

1985   Releases first music video, "Hanky-Panky"; embarks
        on cross-country tour in Canada; premieres in New
        York City at the Bottom Line; signs a three-album
        deal with Sire Records/Warner Brothers; becomes
        songwriting partners with Ben Mink; performs with
        the Edmonton Symphony Orchestra; receives
        Canadian Juno Award for Most Promising Female
        Vocalist

1986   Records *Angel with a Lariat* in England; debuts
        on American television on "Late Night with
        David Letterman"; appears on country show "Hee
        Haw"; opens for country singer Dwight Yoakam
        on tour

1987   Performs at Nashville's Grand Ole Opry; sings duet
        with Roy Orbison on "Crying"; makes first
        appearance on the "Tonight Show with Johnny
        Carson"; wins Juno Award for Best Country Female
        Vocalist; named Entertainer of the Year by the
        Canadian Country Music Association; collaborates
        with legendary country producer Owen Bradley on
        Shadowland and harmonizes with Nashville stars
        Loretta Lynn, Kitty Wells, and Brenda Lee

1988   Headlines the closing ceremonies of the Winter
        Olympics in Calgary, Alberta; guest stars on Orbison's
        HBO special "A Black and White Night"; opens
        for Lyle Lovett on tour; appears on HBO special
        "Country Music: A New Tradition"; receives three
        Grammy nominations and wins Best Country Music
        Collaboration for "Crying"; takes home Entertainer
        of the Year, Best Female Vocalist, and Album of the
        Year (for *Shadowland*) honors at the Canadian
        Country Music Awards; declared Woman of the Year
        by the Canadian women's magazine *Chatelaine*

1989   Wins a Grammy for Best Female Country
        Performance for *Absolute Torch and Twang*; performs at
        Amnesty International Human Rights Now! concert
        in Toronto

1990   Makes public service announcement encouraging
        vegetarianism for People for the Ethical Treatment
        of Animals; named Canada's Female Artist of the

	Decade; participates in AIDS benefit project *Red Hot + Blue*; portrays a lesbian in the movie *Salmonberries*
1992	Officially comes out in an *Advocate* interview; switches from country to pop music on *Ingenue* album; wins Grammy for Best Female Pop Vocalist; receives award as Best New Female Adult Contemporary Artist at the American Music Awards; performs at Concert of Hope AIDS benefit in London
1993	Appears in male drag on the cover of *Vanity Fair*; creates soundtrack for *Even Cowgirls Get the Blues*
1994	Performs at Los Angeles's AIDS Project benefit and New York's LifeBeat AIDS concert; acts in *Teresa's Tattoo*; begins work on next album
1995	Records *all you can eat* in her new studio on her Vancouver farm

FURTHER READING

Bennahum, David. *The k.d. lang Illustrated Biography.* London: Omnibus Press, 1994.

Bennetts, Leslie. "k.d. lang's Edge: Crossing Over, Catching Fire." *Vanity Fair,* August 1993, 94–146.

Bufwack, Mary A., and Robert K. Oermann. *Finding Her Voice: The Saga of Women in Country Music.* New York: Crown, 1993.

Gillmor, Don. "The Reincarnation of Kathryn Dawn Lang." *Saturday Night,* June 1990, 27–35.

lang, k.d. "Lesley Gore on k.d. lang . . . and Vice Versa." *Ms.,* July/August 1990, 30–33.

Lemon, Brendan. "Virgin Territory: Music's Purest Vocalist Opens Up." *Advocate,* June 16, 1992, 34–46.

Magnuson, Ann. "Ann Magnuson Talks While k.d. Croons." *Elle,* May 1992, 80–86.

Mockus, Martha. "Queer Thoughts on Country Music and k.d. lang." In *Queering the Pitch: The New Gay and Lesbian Musicology,* edited by Philip Brett, Elizabeth Wood, and Gary C. Thomas. New York: Routledge, 1994, 257–71.

Philip, Tom, Kenneth Whyte, and Lori Cohen. "The Outrageous K.D. Lang." *Alberta Report,* December 3, 1984, 38–45.

Robertson, William. *k.d. lang: Carrying the Torch.* Toronto: ECW Press, 1992.

Rogers, Ray. "k.d. dawns again." *Out,* Dec./Jan. 1996, 78–86.

Rogers, Sheila. "k.d. lang: Singing into a Mirror." *Musician,* April 1992, 36–43.

Starr, Victoria. *k.d. lang: All You Get Is Me.* New York: St. Martin's Press, 1994.

Udovitch, Mim. "k.d. lang." *Rolling Stone,* August 5, 1993, 54–57.

Walters, Barry. "lang time coming." *The Advocate,* Oct. 17, 1995, 63–64.

INDEX

Paula Martinac is a writer, editor, and activist. Born and raised in Pittsburgh, she has lived in New York City since the early 1980s. She has published two novels, *Home Movies* (1993) and *Out of Time* (1990), which won a Lambda Literary Award for Best Lesbian Fiction, and is at work on a third novel, *Beards*. She coauthored *Voyages Out 1: Lesbian Short Fiction* and was the editor of the anthology *The One You Call Sister: New Women's Fiction* (1989).

Martin Duberman is Distinguished Professor of History at the Graduate Center for the City University of New York and the founder and director of the Center for Lesbian and Gay Studies. One of the country's foremost historians, he is the author of 17 books and numerous articles and essays. He has won the Bancroft Prize for *Charles Francis Adams* (1960); two Lambda awards for *Hidden from History: Reclaiming the Gay and Lesbian Past,* an anthology that he coedited; and a special award from the National Academy of Arts and Letters for his overall "contributions to literature." His play, *In White America,* won the Vernon Rice/Drama Desk Award in 1964. His other works include *James Russell Lowell* (1966), *Black Mountain: An Exploration in Community* (1972), *Paul Robeson* (1989), *Cures: A Gay Man's Odyssey* (1991), *Stonewall* (1993), *Midlife Queer* (1996), and *A Queer World* (1996).

PICTURE CREDITS

AP/Wide World Photos: pp. 30, 69, 74, 76, 87, 100, 117; Archive Photos: pp. 17, 18, 20, 39, 50, 63, 96, 115, 120, 127; Courtesy of the Consort School: pp. 24, 27, 33, 34; *The Edmonton Journal:* pp. 54, 60; The *Edmonton Sun:* pp. 53, 56, 80, 93, 110; Courtesy of Richard Houghton: pp. 36, 42; Courtesy of PETA: p. 90; Photofest: pp. 2, 14, 46, 66, 83, 84, 103, 106, 122; Courtesy of the Public Relations Department of Red Deer College: p. 45; Reuters/Bettmann: p. 95; UPI/Bettmann: p. 71.